RAND NATIONAL DEFENSE RESEARCH INSTITUTE

SimCoach Evaluation

A Virtual Human Intervention to Encourage
Service-Member Help-Seeking for Posttraumatic
Stress Disorder and Depression

Daniella Meeker, Jennifer L. Cerully, Megan D. Johnson, Neema Iyer,
Jeremy R. Kurz, Deborah M. Scharf

Prepared for the Office of the Secretary of Defense
Approved for public release; distribution unlimited

For more information on this publication, visit www.rand.org/t/RR505

Library of Congress Cataloging-in-Publication Data is available for this publication.
ISBN: 978-0-8330-8813-0

Published by the RAND Corporation, Santa Monica, Calif.
© Copyright 2015 RAND Corporation
RAND® is a registered trademark.

Support RAND
Make a tax-deductible charitable contribution at
www.rand.org/giving/contribute

www.rand.org

Preface

As of December 31, 2012, more than 2.5 million service members had served in Operation Enduring Freedom (OEF) or Operation Iraqi Freedom (OIF) (Defense Manpower Data Center, 2013). Compared with service in previous conflicts, service in OEF or OIF is associated with longer deployments, more-frequent deployments, and shorter rest times between deployments (Belasco, 2011; Bruner, 2006; Serafino, 2005). In addition, National Guard and Reserve Component troops have been called on to a greater extent than in past conflicts, with nearly one-third of deployed service members coming from Reserve Components or National Guard (Committee on the Initial Assessment of Readjustment Needs of Military Personnel, Veterans, and Their Families, 2010; Committee on the Assessment of the Readjustment Needs of Military Personnel, Veterans, and Their Families, 2013). As a result of these difficult circumstances, service members supporting OEF or OIF conflicts experience high rates of traumatic brain injury (TBI) and psychological health problems. In response, the U.S. Department of Defense (DoD) has stood up multiple programs to help meet these needs.

In 2009, the Assistant Secretary of Defense for Health Affairs and the Defense Centers of Excellence for Psychological Health and Traumatic Brain Injury (DCoE) asked the RAND National Defense Research Institute to develop a comprehensive catalog of existing programs sponsored or funded by DoD to support psychological health and care for TBI, create tools to support ongoing assessment and evaluation of the DoD portfolio of programs, and conduct evaluations of a subset of these programs.

This report describes our assessment of SimCoach, one of the programs for which DCoE commissioned an evaluation. SimCoach is a computer program designed to encourage service members, especially those with signs or symptoms of posttraumatic stress disorder or depression, to seek help to improve their psychological health. It features a virtual human who speaks and gestures in a video game–like interface. It was created by researchers at the University of Southern California (USC) Institute for Creative Technologies in collaboration with the USC School of Social Work and subject-matter experts and was funded by the Assistant Secretary of Defense for Health Affairs.

This report will be of particular interest to officials within DoD who are responsible for the psychological health and well-being of service members, as well as to others within the military who are developing programs and strategies to encourage service members to seek appropriate psychological health treatment. The contents of this report may also be of interest to officials in the U.S. Department of Veterans Affairs and to veterans service organizations that seek to accomplish the same goals among the veteran population.

This research was sponsored by DCoE and conducted within the Forces and Resources Policy Center of the RAND National Defense Research Institute, a federally funded research and development center sponsored by the Office of the Secretary of Defense, the Joint Staff, the Unified Combatant Commands, the Navy, the Marine Corps, the defense agencies, and the defense Intelligence Community.

For more information on the RAND Forces and Resources Policy Center, see http://www.rand.org/nsrd/ndri/centers/frp.html or contact the director (contact information is provided on the web page). This report is one of a series of program evaluations conducted as part of the "Innovative Practices for Psychological Health and Traumatic Brain Injury" project; for more information and to access other products from this project, please visit the project web page (http://www.rand.org/multi/military/innovative-practices.html).

Contents

Figures and Tables

Figures

Tables

Executive Summary

This report describes our assessment of SimCoach, a computer program featuring a virtual human who speaks and gestures in a video game–like interface, designed to encourage service members, especially those with signs or symptoms of posttraumatic stress disorder (PTSD) or depression, to seek help to improve their psychological health.

Background

As of December 31, 2012, more than 2.5 million service members had served in Operation Enduring Freedom (OEF) or Operation Iraqi Freedom (OIF) (Defense Manpower Data Center, 2013). Estimates suggest that approximately 18.5 percent of combat troops returning from these conflicts meet structured survey criteria for PTSD or depression (Tanielian and Jaycox, 2008). Many also experienced traumatic brain injuries (TBIs) from blasts associated with improvised explosive devices, the signature injury of the OEF and OIF conflicts. TBIs and psychological health problems often occur within the same person and can complicate the course of these conditions (Bryan and Clemans, 2013; Barnes, Walter, and Chard, 2012; Hoge, McGurk, et al., 2008).

Despite several initiatives to address their psychological health needs, service members often experience barriers to treatment, including concerns about stigma or threats to career advancement (Hoge, Castro, et al., 2004; Pietrzak et al., 2009; Vogt, 2011; Tanielian and Jaycox, 2008). Innovative solutions are needed to increase rates at which service members and their families appropriately access and use mental health care for psychological health conditions and TBI.

The Defense Centers of Excellence for Psychological Health and Traumatic Brain Injury (DCoE) has funded several such programs, including SimCoach. SimCoach is a virtual-reality (VR) platform that allows users to interact anonymously with virtual humans in online environments; as such, they can use the platform to access helpful information about psychological health and TBI services without privacy concerns. An online, VR intervention may be particularly appealing and efficacious for service members because (1) many people turn first to the Internet to answer psychological health questions, (2) the novelty of the intervention may render it engaging, and (3) it allows for anonymity of users in a context in which they may be hesitant to be identified. However, little empirical research has tested these hypotheses about online VR interventions for service members seeking help for psychological health concerns directly, and whether SimCoach itself is acceptable and effective for promoting help-seeking is unknown.

In this report, we describe our assessment of the first public release of SimCoach (SimCoach Beta). The aim of this evaluation was to document and assess SimCoach development procedures and then test and report the program's efficacy for promoting help-seeking for signs and symptoms of PTSD and depression among service members. The evaluation design included two components. First, we conducted a formative evaluation to describe SimCoach's design and content relative to established best practices in software development and clinical intervention development. Second, we conducted a summative evaluation in which we used a randomized controlled trial (RCT) to test SimCoach Beta's efficacy in increasing participants' intention to seek treatment relative to that of controls. This report summarizes the results of the formative and summative evaluation efforts and makes recommendations to SimCoach developers and developers of similar interventions, as well as policymakers who invest in the development of VR interventions for service members' psychological health.

Evaluation Methods

Formative Evaluation

In the formative evaluation, we collected data in interviews with SimCoach developers, published and supporting materials provided by the SimCoach team, and direct assessment of the SimCoach Beta interface. These data were used to compare the development process with best practices for software engineering and development of behavioral interventions. We reviewed the SimCoach Beta interface for content and features, assessing consistency with established evidence and best practices for conducting surveys among participants at risk for distress.

Summative Evaluation

Study participants interacted with the SimCoach Beta program's virtual human. Interactions with the virtual human included conversational dialogue prior to the administration of one of two adapted instruments for assessing psychological health—the PTSD Checklist (PCL) and the nine-item Patient Health Questionnaire (PHQ-9)—followed by personalized recommendations. Participants for the RCT were recruited online from Google ads and websites and email lists targeting service members. The RCT compared help-seeking outcomes across three study arms: (1) the SimCoach arm, in which respondents were administered questionnaires of outcome measures after interacting with the SimCoach Beta tool, (2) a content-matched control arm identical to the SimCoach arm but substituting the virtual human interactions with conventional online text-based methods, and (3) a no-treatment control arm in which participants completed the outcome assessments without any additional assessments or recommendations. The primary outcome measure was the intention to seek help for PTSD or depression, with secondary outcomes related to perceived barriers to seeking and accessing care.

Evaluation Findings

Formative Evaluation

The formative evaluation showed that SimCoach Beta (the version included in the summative evaluation RCT) was reliable and that the technical development approach was consistent with software development best practices, with a scalable architecture and iterative development strategy incorporating multiple rounds of user feedback (Scott et al., 2011).

Our assessment of SimCoach Beta's clinical intervention content was aligned with best practices insofar as the developers established a panel of reputable domain experts from the earliest stages to inform development. However, our review of SimCoach Beta content indicated that the personalized recommendations that the program offered were less well-developed. For instance, we identified cases in which the program directed users to web pages that did not mention treatment or help-seeking. In reviewing program responses to text entries indicating user distress, we also found that the list of phrases that would trigger directions to seek help was limited such that some user expressions of distress might not trigger an appropriate referral to help or emergency services. Other technical limitations of the program were that it employed adapted, "conversational" versions of standardized screening measures for depression and PTSD that have not been fully validated and that many users responding to online advertisements during pilot-testing were attempting to access SimCoach Beta from mobile platforms that the program did not support.

The main finding from the formative evaluation is that SimCoach Beta testing had a much greater focus on user experiences than on the outcome of interest for our study—the program's efficacy in improving users' intentions to seek help. This focus on user experience was reflected in our findings from the summative evaluation.

Summative Evaluation

Our summative evaluation assessed help-seeking outcomes, perceptions of barriers to help-seeking, and user experience among SimCoach Beta users compared with experiences of controls who received a text-based version of the SimCoach Beta intervention (content-matched but no interaction with a virtual-human element) and with a no-treatment control consisting of outcome assessments only. Of the 1,362 users who accessed the initial screener, 557 were found eligible and randomized to one of the three arms. Of those who were randomized, 280 completed the full trial and survey. We did not detect a significant effect of the SimCoach Beta intervention on help-seeking intentions compared with participants receiving no intervention.

Recommendations

Our evaluation was based on one version, the first public release (SimCoach Beta), which was intended to be improved upon and extended. As a result, we provide two sets of recommendations: one for SimCoach developers and one for DCoE, which funded SimCoach development.

We recommend that SimCoach developers do the following:

- Implement best practices for the development of help-seeking interventions.
- Given user reluctance to interact with a virtual human, consider new approaches to Sim-Coach marketing to promote the value of the approach.
- Use validated screening instruments when possible to ensure that these instruments have sufficient reliability, sensitivity, and specificity.
- Consider using an outcome-oriented, iterative development process during subsequent improvements to the SimCoach intervention.

- Continue to design new dialogue and content to meet SimCoach goals of reaching a target audience of service members, veterans, and family members.
- If future versions are found to be effective, develop versions of SimCoach that are compatible with mobile devices and web browsers.
- Consider using SimCoach in other cases in which potentially sensitive questionnaires and information may be delivered.

Our results do not show any conclusive evidence of the efficacy of SimCoach Beta. In that light, we offer the following recommendations to guide further decisions about DCoE's involvement with SimCoach and similar programs:

- Consider changing funding models to motivate best practices in intervention development. For example, DCoE could consider requiring submission of pilot data prior to funding larger technology-development projects or requiring the use of validated instruments.
- Support pilot evaluations and dissemination approaches in different contexts.
- Consider investing in strategies to guide the development of technology-based clinical interventions.
- DCoE might play an active role in design and monitoring of outcome-oriented progress metrics for technology-development projects.

Conclusions

Technology-driven behavioral interventions, such as SimCoach, are being widely and rapidly developed and disseminated, yet there is no established set of best practices that marries technology development and the development of interventions to improve psychological health. Although SimCoach Beta software development was consistent with DoD best practices (Scott et al., 2011) and the results of the study suggest that users had a satisfactory experience while using SimCoach Beta, participants in the RCT did not show greater intentions to seek help than users who did not receive any questionnaires or recommendations. It is possible that an outcome-oriented approach to developing software for behavioral change over a user experience–oriented approach might be preferable in this particular domain of interventions. Stakeholders in SimCoach and other technology-driven behavioral interventions might consider coordinating a consensus process for creating best practices and principles for future reference.

Acknowledgments

We gratefully acknowledge the support of our current and former project monitors, Yoni Tyberg, CAPT John Golden, and Col. Christopher Robinson, and current and former staff at the Defense Centers of Excellence for Psychological Health and Traumatic Brain Injury. We also acknowledge the support and cooperation of the SimCoach development team at the University of Southern California, including the principal investigator, Albert "Skip" Rizzo, and other members of the team: Josh Williams, Eric Forbell, Belinda Lange, and Sin-Hwa Kang. We appreciate the comments provided by two reviewers, Lisa H. Jaycox and Tracy Stecker, on this and earlier drafts. Their critiques, provided as part of the RAND quality assurance process, improved the quality of this report. We also appreciate the assistance provided by Paul Steinberg in writing this report. We are also grateful to the service members who participated in our study for taking the time and effort to do so.

Abbreviations

BML   Behavior Markup Language

CI   confidence interval

DCoE   Defense Centers of Excellence for Psychological Health and Traumatic Brain Injury

DM   dialogue management

DoD   U.S. Department of Defense

DTIC   Defense Technical Information Center

FLoReS   Forward-Looking, Reward Seeking

ICT   Institute for Creative Technologies

IP   Internet protocol

MDD   major depressive disorder

mxNLU   maximum-likelihood natural-language understanding

NLU   natural-language understanding

NVBG   NonVerbal Behavior Generator

OEF   Operation Enduring Freedom

OIF   Operation Iraqi Freedom

PCL   PTSD Checklist

PHQ-2   two-item Patient Health Questionnaire

PHQ-9   nine-item Patient Health Questionnaire

PLISSIT   Permission, Limited Information, Specific Suggestions, and Intensive Therapy

PTSD   posttraumatic stress disorder

RCT   randomized controlled trial

SBIRT   screening, brief intervention, and referral to treatment

SCXML   state chart extensible markup language

SME   subject-matter expert

TBI   traumatic brain injury

USC   University of Southern California

VA   U.S. Department of Veterans Affairs

VR   virtual reality

CHAPTER ONE

Introduction

Background

Epidemiology of Posttraumatic Stress Disorder and Depression Among Service Members

As of December 31, 2012, more than 2.5 million service members had served in Operation Enduring Freedom (OEF) or Operation Iraqi Freedom (OIF) (Defense Manpower Data Center, 2013). Compared with that in previous conflicts, service in OEF or OIF bears some unique characteristics, including longer deployments, more-frequent deployments, and shorter rest times between deployments (Belasco, 2011; Bruner, 2006; Serafino, 2005). National Guard and Reserve Component troops have also been called on to a greater extent than in past conflicts, with nearly one-third of deployed service members coming from Reserve Components or National Guard (Committee on the Initial Assessment of Readjustment Needs of Military Personnel, Veterans, and Their Families, 2010; Committee on the Assessment of the Readjustment Needs of Military Personnel, Veterans, and Their Families, 2013).

Service members are experiencing extreme traumas in these conflicts, including roadside bombs, suicide bombs, improvised explosive devices, handling of human remains, and extreme violence. Exposure to all of these types of trauma increases the risk for posttraumatic stress disorder (PTSD) and depression (Tanielian and Jaycox, 2008; Committee on the Initial Assessment of Readjustment Needs of Military Personnel, Veterans, and Their Families, 2010; Committee on the Assessment of the Readjustment Needs of Military Personnel, Veterans, and Their Families, 2013).

Estimates suggest that approximately 7 percent to 20 percent of combat troops returning home from OEF and OIF conflicts meet structured survey criteria for PTSD (Hoge, Castro, et al., 2004; Ramchand et al., 2010; Seal et al., 2007; Smith et al., 2008; Tanielian and Jaycox, 2008; Vasterling et al., 2010). Many also experienced traumatic brain injuries (TBIs) from blasts; indeed, TBI has been called the signature injury of the OEF and OIF conflicts. TBIs and psychological health problems often occur within the same person and can complicate the course of these conditions (Bryan and Clemans, 2013; Barnes, Walter, and Chard, 2012; Hoge, McGurk, et al., 2008).

Barriers to Psychological Health Care Among Service Members

Although mental health disorders, especially PTSD and depression, are common among service members, not all service members who need treatment receive it (Hoge, Auchterlonie, and Milliken, 2006; Shiner, 2011; Tanielian and Jaycox, 2008). Service members experience a wide variety of barriers to help-seeking, including concerns about harm to one's career or losing the respect of one's own commander or supervisor (Hoge, Castro, et al., 2004; Kim et al., 2011;

Pietrzak et al., 2009; Tanielian and Jaycox, 2008); concerns about being distrusted or treated differently by peers, representing a fear of being stigmatized by others for having a mental health problem or seeking treatment for it (Hoge, Castro, et al., 2004; Pietrzak et al., 2009); negative beliefs about mental health treatment, such as believing that mental health care is ineffective or not trusting mental health professionals (Hoge, Castro, et al., 2004; Kim et al., 2011; Pietrzak et al., 2009; Vogt, 2011); and having difficulty admitting to a problem, asking for help, or talking about mental health problems (e.g., in the case of PTSD, having difficulty talking about trauma) (Stecker, Shiner, et al., 2013; Stecker, Fortney, et al., 2007). Logistical barriers to care, such as having difficulty getting time off work or paying for mental health care, can also interfere with treatment-seeking and receipt of appropriate services (Kim et al., 2011; Hoge, Castro, et al., 2004; Tanielian and Jaycox, 2008; Vogt et al., 2006).

Technology Solutions to Improve Help-Seeking

A significant amount of research has explored technology's potential to enhance the delivery of mental health treatment, with a systematic review identifying more than 40 studies using Internet-based technology to address mental health problems related to traumatic stress (Amstadter et al., 2009). However, there has been less research evaluating technological interventions to identify people at risk for mental health problems or to promote help-seeking. Published studies on these topics are focused largely on nonmilitary populations and the identification of and early intervention for substance-use problems (Community Preventive Services Task Force, 2013).

Using a technology-based approach to identify service members and veterans who are experiencing mental health problems and to encourage help-seeking may be fruitful for several reasons. First, a screening, brief intervention, and referral to treatment (SBIRT) approach is an evidence-based strategy to promote help-seeking for people who need it ("Screening, Brief Intervention and Referral to Treatment (SBIRT) in Behavioral Healthcare," 2011), although more evidence is needed to assess the efficacy of this approach for depression and trauma and anxiety disorders. Screening with brief intervention has been successfully implemented online and is recommended for use to address excessive alcohol consumption (Community Preventive Services Task Force, 2013); however, evidence for depression and trauma or anxiety SBIRT is not available. Second, technology-based interventions can allow users to access information and services anonymously and easily, thus potentially addressing the privacy concerns and logistic barriers to care identified among military service members. Third, military service members and veterans are already likely to look for health information online and to be comfortable using technology (Houston et al., 2013; Orvis et al., 2010), suggesting that technology-based interventions would be feasible and acceptable to a military population.

Overview of the SimCoach Program

SimCoach is an "intelligent, interactive, online virtual human healthcare guide" (University of Southern California [USC] Institute for Creative Technologies [ICT], undated) designed to encourage service members to "take the first step and seek information and advice with regard to their healthcare (e.g. psychological health, . . .), and their general personal welfare" (ICT, undated). SimCoach features a virtual human who speaks and gestures in a chat-like interface (see Figure 1.1). When responding to the questions asked by SimCoach, users can choose to use standard responses from drop-down menus or compose their own text entries. SimCoach then responds in writing, with an option for responses to be spoken aloud. The SimCoach

Figure 1.1
Screenshot of SimCoach

SOURCE: USC ICT. Used with permission.
RAND *RR505-1.1*

program administers screening tools for PTSD and depression in a conversational manner, generating behavioral recommendations with links to accompanying online articles specific to each depression or PTSD symptom the user endorses. SimCoach is designed to be accessed anonymously through the Internet, thus allowing service members to obtain information and self-assessment without disclosure to other service members or commanding officers.

SimCoach is the first online psychological health intervention designed to promote help-seeking and information-gathering using virtual-reality (VR) avatars. Using this novel technology, SimCoach is intended to provide service members with reliable, educational resources tailored to their needs, thereby avoiding the risk of potential "information overload" that can accompany a traditional Internet search. SimCoach is available online to anyone, and it is free of charge. It does not require the user to download any software or log in to an account. Because the only necessary equipment is a computer with an Internet connection, SimCoach can be used virtually anywhere in the world, including deployed locations, and, because users can choose to have SimCoach interact silently through the chat box, they can use the program discreetly in a public location. Indeed, because SimCoach is completely anonymous, does not record identifiable information, add it to a medical record, or make information accessible to users' chain of command, it has potential to overcome some stigma-related barriers to accessing care.

Informed by descriptions provided by SimCoach developers in interviews and documents, we created a logic model detailing the structures and mechanisms by which SimCoach might affect seeking help and perceived barriers to care and, ultimately, engagement in treatment and improved psychological health and well-being (Figure 1.2).

User interactions with SimCoach involve a sequence of steps that requires increasing levels of engagement with the program. First, SimCoach must attract and engage the user

Figure 1.2
Inferred SimCoach Intervention Logic Model

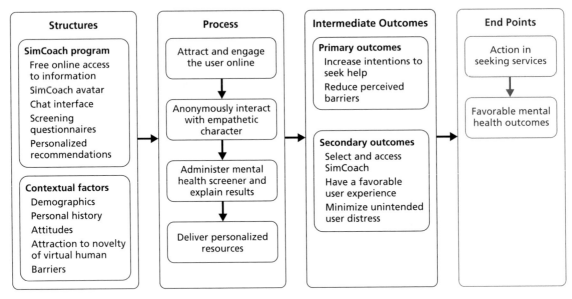

online in an environment in which there are many other competing options (Liu, White, and Dumais, 2010). After initial engagement, the initial dialogue with the virtual human character (e.g., "Bill Ford," the avatar depicted in Figure 1.1) must further draw the user into an experience that is both interesting and comfortable. Third, the virtual human administers a questionnaire that is scored in real time to provide the user with an explanation of results that raises his or her awareness about his or her psychological health symptoms. Finally, the user must remain engaged to receive, consider, and then act on personalized resources and recommendations for actions. SimCoach, as currently conceived, is not intended to deliver psychological health services.

The Defense Centers of Excellence for Psychological Health and Traumatic Brain Injury (DCoE) initiated SimCoach development. DCoE directly approached the USC ICT, which collaborated with the USC School of Social Work and a team of subject-matter experts (SMEs) to develop requirements and measures for the simulated speech and appearance of virtual humans. Albert "Skip" Rizzo, Ph.D., is the principal investigator.

Objectives and Approach

The Assistant Secretary of Defense for Health Affairs and DCoE asked the RAND Corporation to conduct an evaluation of SimCoach. The evaluation was guided by the following aims:

- Document and describe the development of an avatar to conduct mental health screening and provide relevant resources and recommendations.
- Assess user reactions to the interface, resources, and recommendations.
- Test SimCoach's efficacy for increasing intentions to seek psychological services.

The RAND team took a two-phased approach to meeting these aims (see Figure 1.3). The first phase was a *formative evaluation* of the design, development, and implementation of the first public release of the SimCoach program (SimCoach Beta). The aims of the formative evaluation were to thoroughly characterize SimCoach design and development and to inform implementation of a rigorous outcome evaluation. The formative evaluation involved qualitative analysis of several sources of information, including SimCoach documentation, interviews, and data provided by SimCoach designers; SimCoach content; and results from pilot tests. These data were used to assess adherence to best practices for software development and clinical referral interventions, as well as technical implementations and safety to human subjects relevant to the implementation of the randomized controlled trial (RCT) in the summative evaluation. Evaluation metrics and benchmarks are detailed in Table 1.1.

The *summative evaluation* tested SimCoach Beta efficacy and user experience with an online RCT and survey to assess the intermediate outcomes of the project: increased intentions to seek help and reduced perceptions of barriers to care. The RCT was aimed to replicate the intended use environment and audience for SimCoach; as such, participants were recruited online rather than in military or clinical settings. Specifically, the RCT compared efficacy and user experience outcomes for users in three study arms. The first arm used SimCoach; the second arm presented the same content as SimCoach but in conventional online forms rather than by a virtual human; and the third group, a nontreatment group, did not receive this treatment before the efficacy assessment. Secondary outcomes of the summative evaluation included the experiences of SimCoach Beta users compared with those of controls using and receiving information via more-traditional channels.

Figure 1.3
Evaluation Design

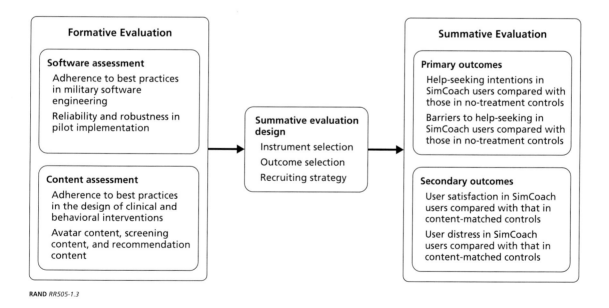

Table 1.1
Evaluation Benchmarks and Metrics

Evaluation Component	Evaluation Benchmark or Metric	Data Source
Formative evaluation		
Technology	DoD software development best practices (Scott et al., 2011)	Documentation, interviews
	Technical implementation	Direct evaluation
Intervention	Intervention design best practices (Campbell et al., 2000)	Documentation, direct evaluation
Summative evaluation		
Efficacy	Intention to seek help (Wilson, Deane, and Ciarrochi, 2005)	Randomized user survey
	Barriers to seeking care (Britt et al., 2008)	Randomized user survey
User experience	User experience data (SimCoach Team in MedVR Group, 2012)	Randomized and self-selected
	User distress questionnaire	Randomized and self-selected

NOTE: DoD = U.S. Department of Defense.

Organization of This Report

In what follows, we provide additional detail about how SimCoach was assessed and the results of those assessments. Specifically, Chapter Two describes the formative evaluation of the Sim-Coach Beta design and development process. Chapter Three details the approach and results of an RCT designed to test the efficacy of SimCoach Beta in increasing help-seeking intentions and usability. Finally, in Chapter Four, we summarize the key findings of our evaluation and provide recommendations to key stakeholders of the program, including its developers and the policymakers who initiated and funded the research.

CHAPTER TWO

Formative Evaluation

We designed our formative evaluation to assess two components of the SimCoach program: (1) the SimCoach software platform and (2) the clinical content in the version of SimCoach we evaluated—a beta version aimed at service members that included content related to depression and PTSD. The SimCoach version evaluated was the version in release in December 2011. We took this approach because SimCoach is an ambitious software development project worthy of separate assessment from the content associated with the particular version of the intervention we evaluated. This approach also facilitated a more rigorous design and implementation of the summative (outcome) evaluation described in Chapter Three.

Software Assessment

In this section, we first provide an overview of the software, describe the method and results of software pilot-testing, and compare the SimCoach development processes with identified best practices in military software development. Data sources for this evaluation include documentation and data provided by the SimCoach development team, publicly available documentation, and results of internal and pilot-testing of the beta version of the software. This section of the report assumes that the reader has basic familiarity with software development principles.

Software Overview

ICT's virtual human architecture is an ongoing project that has supported a wide variety of predecessors to SimCoach. The existing suite of tools includes a variety of components that support the intelligent behaviors of virtual humans (Morie et al., 2012). SimCoach is built on a highly customizable platform with a flexible authoring interface that is intended to enable rapid development of new characters and environments. Developers anticipated a scalable system, with users ultimately being able to choose from several different avatars of different races, genders, and military service history, or even civilian applications. This variation is intended to allow for a more personalized experience to enhance users' comfort with the SimCoach interaction. SimCoach developers built a system intended to allow providers to author new content for the program (e.g., adding screening tools for other mental and physical health challenges), with the intent of creating a continuously improving platform. In the words of the developers,

> The software principle underlying design of SimCoach is to create a backbone that can grow organically over time and does not tie the government to a single developer. We will design the software to be open, modular, and easy to extend and author content. Where possible, the system will incorporate open source modules and open standards to facilitate

incorporation in a modular fashion to facilitate incorporation of the latest advances. . . . A series of content development tools will facilitate the creation of new virtual human characters by non-technical clinicians [so] that the system can grow and expand over time with new experts and focus areas as required. (Rizzo, Gratch, et al., 2009)

The authoring interface, currently referred to as *Roundtable*, is a graphical user interface that facilitates the development of content and characters. Limited documentation of the tool is available and is expected to be described in more detail in Swartout et al. (2013). Tutorials are also available online.

Figure 2.1 provides a simplified view of the SimCoach artificial intelligence architecture that executes content developed with SimCoach authoring tools. Specifically, the technology behind SimCoach is based on a modular architecture that allows for different steps in the interaction process to be implemented with different underlying components. Different algorithms and developer-authored content can be substituted for the various artificial intelligence processing steps in the virtual human so that the system can constantly be improved with state-of-the-art algorithms. The information flow begins with a typed user utterance that is then handled by a natural-language understanding (NLU) process. Currently, an algorithm based on a maximum-likelihood NLU (mxNLU) process parses the user input into predefined user speech act representations that are defined during a system authoring phase that is specific to each intervention instance (Sagae et al., 2009). These representations are passed to a dialogue management (DM) module. The DM module executes rules for generating appropriate responses to user input. The algorithms for driving this might be defined based on rules that are dictated during scenario authoring (as is the case in the original version of SimCoach) or based on a combination of dictated rules and "learned" rules that are generated by example. (An alternative version, the Forward-Looking, Reward Seeking DM, is being tested [Morbini et al., 2012]). The response is passed to the NonVerbal Behavior Generator (NVBG), which passes computable specifications for avatar behavior in Behavior Markup Language (BML) to an animation control system. According to recent documentation (Morie et al., 2012), Sim-Coach uses the ICT SmartBody system (Thiebaux et al., 2008) to achieve animation control specifications that are sent to real-time graphics rendering engines.

Figure 2.1
SimCoach Response Pipeline Technology

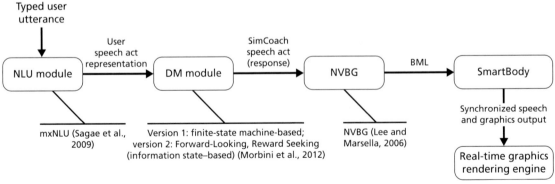

Pilot-Testing

The SimCoach developers implemented an instance of SimCoach Beta hosted at ICT for use in our evaluation. We tested this instance internally and pilot-tested it with 40 participants recruited with Google ads. Our tests showed that SimCoach Beta performed reliably across a variety of connection speeds and browser platforms, loading smoothly without crashing or long delays. During pilot-testing, a large portion of people who clicked on recruiting links directed at service members with psychological health concerns were accessing the survey using mobile devices. Because SimCoach Beta is not compatible with mobile operating systems, we implemented a message directing these users to visit from other devices and, where possible, limited our recruiting advertisements to display only on nonmobile platforms. Issues related to content are described later in this chapter.

Technology Evaluation Methods

In addition to the pilot-testing conducted, we assessed how the SimCoach development process compared with best practices for military software development provided by the chief information officer of DoD (Scott et al., 2011). From this report, we identified the following technical criteria as relevant to SimCoach:

- *flexibility:* Develop components that can be used in a variety of ways.
- *portability:* Develop components that can be used on multiple platforms.
- *modularity:* Develop components that are modular (e.g., with clearly defined subcomponents and perhaps support for a "plug-in" architecture).
- *use of open standards:* Where possible, avoid depending on interfaces that are controlled by a single vendor.
- *software reuse and collaboration with existing projects:* A project should focus on building new software, not reimplementing projects that already exist.
- *avoiding dependencies on non-open standards:* Depend only on widely used platforms, libraries, and development tools; if a proprietary component must be depended on, isolate it through plug-ins or an interface defined by an open standard.
- *applying rapid development cycles with iterative evaluations:* Develop, test, and update versions in response to feedback from an increasing scope of target users.
- *findability:* Software, documentation, and related resources should be easily discoverable by intended users.

Technology Evaluation Results

Table 2.1 summarizes our comparison of the SimCoach development process and the DoD criteria listed above. SimCoach was developed from a suite of tools designed for flexibility in use. Although the program is portable in its ability to be invoked by other applications, at the time of the evaluation, it could not be accessed on iOS mobile platforms. SimCoach adheres to the DoD modularity and reuse criteria, which advise that programs be modular (can be easily substituted across different implementations and separated from the program or software system as a whole) and reusable (can be easily incorporated in new programs or software systems)—SimCoach programs were based on modifications of software modules previously developed in related work. Although standards for virtual-human technologies are still evolving, SimCoach aligns with best practices in open standards in its underlying technologies (e.g., BML native to the SmartBody control system). The developers have limited dependencies on proprietary

Table 2.1
Alignment of SimCoach Technology with Best Practices

Best Practice	Measure	SimCoach
Flexibility	Can SimCoach or parts of the SimCoach system be used in a variety of ways and have more potential users (i.e., the developers using the ICT Virtual Human Toolkit) to aid the project?	The SimCoach project is based on a suite of tools that have been developed and curated with the intent of flexible use. A significant contribution of the SimCoach development effort to the technologies in the ICT Virtual Human Toolkit is the "service-ization" of tools to facilitate more-flexible implementations. Service-ization of tools involves creating more-modular, portable versions of programs that work in multiple contexts. The ICT Virtual Human Toolkit programs can be invoked by other applications and return results that generalize beyond SimCoach, meeting this best-practice criterion.
Portability	Can SimCoach be used on multiple platforms? A component is portable if it can be used on more platforms, allowing for more potential users.	The SimCoach tool is the first in its class to be deployed using the Internet, allowing a wide range of users to access the SimCoach interventions via multiple web browsers. SimCoach was not designed to be accessed on iOS mobile platforms; however, our pilot-testing indicated that many potential users responding to online ads were accessing through mobile devices.
Modularity	Does SimCoach lend itself to a modular, plug-in architecture? A component that is modular is flexible, can be updated more easily than a nonmodular component, can be independently evaluated for correctness, and integrate with other systems without understanding the overall system of which it is a part.	As shown in Morbini et al. (2012), modularity is a strong point of the system. The current version allows plug-ins for human characters, content, and artificial intelligence algorithms. Several of these modules have been separately evaluated in formal or formative processes.
Use of open standards	What open standards does SimCoach use? Open standards are publicly available programming languages, semantic structures, and other tools that do not require proprietary licenses.	Standards are still evolving for virtual human technologies. SimCoach has continued to employ standards in underlying technologies, such as BML native to the SmartBody control system and state chart extensible markup language, to represent the rules employed in the original version of the DM module (Kenny et al., 2007). Furthermore, developers committed to use standard enterprise platforms (J2EE, .NET) for developing component services (Rizzo, Gratch, et al., 2009)
Reuse of and collaboration with existing projects	What existing software components did SimCoach employ?	As described above, SimCoach developers have reused and extended several existing software components curated by ICT. Specifically, SimCoach reuses the NVBG and the SmartBody animation control system.
Avoiding dependencies on proprietary components	Are proprietary components of SimCoach isolated through plug-ins or an interface defined by an open standard?	Proprietary components (for example, three-dimensional rendering engines) are treated as plug-ins to the SmartBody module. As plug-ins, these proprietary components can be substituted with open-source components without significantly altering the rest of the SimCoach codebase if alternatives become available.
Applying rapid development cycles with iterative evaluations	Did SimCoach developers develop content and applications iteratively? Rapid development cycles involve making incremental changes and receiving feedback from clients and users at very short intervals (e.g., two weeks) rather than working without feedback for extended periods of time.	SimCoach developers conducted several rounds of evaluations and modifications based on feedback from users (SimCoach Team in MedVR Group, 2012).

Table 2.1—Continued

Best Practice	Measure	SimCoach
Findability	Is SimCoach readily discoverable online?	SimCoach developers have made substantial efforts to publicize at even extremely early phases of the project, including through recommended channels, such as press releases and the Defense Technical Information Center. However, online presence might be extended more broadly in the future.

components by treating any proprietary component as a plug-in to allow substitution with an open-source component if such an alternative becomes available. There is evidence that the SimCoach developers applied rapid development cycles with iterative evaluations (SimCoach Team in MedVR Group, 2012). Finally, because SimCoach is at an early stage in its development, it is difficult to judge how it fares on DoD's findability criterion, which is typically assessed by an established online presence. Although the application has been well publicized in academic and domain literature, it has only recently been made available for public use through BraveHeart: Welcome Back Veterans Southeast Initiative and through USC ICT. Technical documentation directly related to SimCoach was not readily found, but it may be premature at this phase of development. SimCoach is based on the ICT Virtual Human Toolkit, which does have an active user community, documentation, and resources.

Formative Evaluation of Development of SimCoach's Behavioral Health Intervention

The evaluation team assessed SimCoach Beta intervention content by reviewing written documentation provided by the SimCoach team (Morbini et al., 2012; Rizzo, Sagae, et al., 2011; Rizzo, Gratch, et al., 2009; John et al., 2011; Rizzo, Buckwalter, et al., 2013; Swartout et al., 2013; Rizzo, Lange, et al., 2011). The evaluation team communicated with the SimCoach team for clarification or questions as needed; however, we did not conduct formal, structured, qualitative interviews with the SimCoach team. In what follows, we first compare the development process and best practices in behavioral health intervention development. We then provide an assessment of the components of SimCoach's behavioral intervention.

Overview of the SimCoach Framework for Intervention Development

In proposal materials, the SimCoach team describes five frameworks as informing the development of the SimCoach intervention (Rizzo, Gratch, et al., 2009): (1) the Permission, Limited Information, Specific Suggestions, and Intensive Therapy (PLISSIT) framework (which has been applied to other stigmatized conditions) (Annon, 1976); (2) the transtheoretical model of behavior change (Miller and Rollnick, 1991); (3) Bright IDEAS (identify a solvable problem, develop possible solutions, evaluate options, act on the plan, and see whether it worked) (interactive pedagogical drama for health interventions; Marsella, Johnson, and LaBore, 2003); (4) social work practice; and (5) entertainment and game practice. No references were provided for the last two models. Although the concepts from these models informed development, SimCoach materials did not describe a concrete logic model that was applied during intervention development. Thus, we selected a general framework for the formative evaluation of intervention development.

Methods: Comparing SimCoach Intervention Development and Best Practices

In this section, we detail best practices in health behavior change intervention development and then compare the SimCoach development process and these best practices (Table 2.2). The SimCoach team did not provide materials with an explicit model for the process by which the intervention was intended to influence outcomes, so we inferred the process (depicted in Figure 2.2). Interventions that aim to change behavior (such as help-seeking) are often complex and involve a variety of components. A phased approach (see Figure 2.2) to intervention development that builds on behavioral theory and evidence-based interventions can optimize

Table 2.2
SimCoach Alignment with Best Practices for Intervention Design and Development

Best Practice from Campbell et al. (2000)	Evaluated Version of SimCoach (SimCoach Beta)
Identify relevant theory to guide intervention development	PLISSIT (Annon, 1976, 1981) Transtheoretical model (Miller and Rollnick, 1991; Prochaska and DiClemente, 1982) Interactive pedagogical drama and Bright IDEAS (Marsella, Johnson, and LaBore, 2003) Social work practice (no reference cited by SimCoach) Entertainment and game practice (no reference cited by SimCoach)
Identify the components of the intervention and the mechanisms by which they are expected to influence outcomes	Not available
Inform intervention components by previous empirical evidence	Adapted "conversational" versions of PHQ-9 and PCL-M[a]
Use expert consensus to guide intervention development when evidence is lacking	SimCoach team used SMEs to guide SimCoach responses to respondent screening measures:[b] • Barbara Olasov Rothbaum, clinical psychologist and professor in the Department of Psychiatry and Behavioral Sciences and director of the Trauma and Anxiety Recovery Program at Emory School of Medicine • JoAnn Difede, attending psychologist at the NewYork-Presbyterian Hospital/Weill Cornell Medical Center, professor in the Department of Psychiatry at Weill Medical College of Cornell University, and director of the Program for Anxiety and Trauma Stress Studies • Bonnie Kennedy, chief science officer at Blue Marble Game Company • Patrick S. Bordnick, associate professor in the University of Houston–Graduate College of Social Work • Kristine Nowak, associate professor in the University of Connecticut Department of Communication • Raymond M. Scurfield, professor emeritus in the University of Southern Mississippi School of Social Work • Benjamin C. Lok, associate professor in the University of Florida College of Engineering • Josef I. Ruzek, clinical psychologist in the VA Palo Alto Health Care System and director of the Dissemination and Training Division of the National Center for Post-Traumatic Stress Disorder
Perform iterative exploratory trials examining the intervention's effect on outcomes	Iterative pilot trials focused on user experience, not on help-seeking outcomes

NOTE: PHQ-9 = nine-item Patient Health Questionnaire. PCL-M = PTSD Checklist, military version. VA = U.S. Department of Veterans Affairs.

[a] Investigators conducted systematic validity and reliability assessment of virtual human modality and conversational adaptation of the PHQ-9 but found the conversational version less reliable than the standard version (John et al., 2011).

[b] SME affiliations were current as of May 20, 2013.

Figure 2.2
Best Practices for Developing Health Behavior Change
Interventions

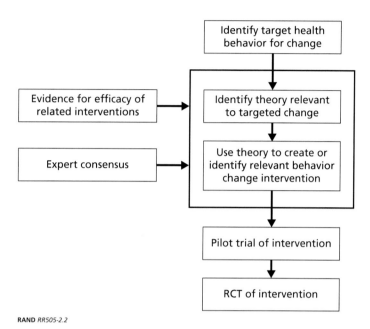

RAND *RR505-2.2*

the effectiveness of such complex interventions (Campbell et al., 2000). In the first phase, the targeted behavior (e.g., help-seeking) is identified. In the second phase, a relevant theory of health behavior change is identified. Third, guided by the selected theory, an appropriate intervention (or combination of interventions) is selected, based on evidence from trials of interventions for related behaviors or populations. When evidence for interventions is lacking, expert consensus is an accepted method for identifying appropriate approaches (Dy et al., 2011). In the fourth phase, hypotheses are developed about the mechanism by which the intervention components will influence outcomes. Fifth, an exploratory trial is conducted, often comparing the intervention and an appropriate alternative. Sixth, results from exploratory trials can be used to modify the intervention prior to a definitive RCT comparing the fully defined intervention and an alternative.

Results: Comparison of SimCoach Beta Behavioral Intervention and Best Practices

The SimCoach developers described their intervention development process as follows: "utterances were developed with Subject Matter Expert (SME) feedback then iteratively refined on the basis of user feedback, and the same SMEs recommended the links to particular forums during focus group review of the interaction." Our assessment of SimCoach alignment with best practices appears in Table 2.2. The SimCoach development process approached best practice in identifying a variety of relevant theories to guide intervention development, but the SimCoach team did not specify how the elements of the relevant theories would be combined. Best practices were not adhered to in identifying the components of the intervention and the mechanisms by which they are expected to influence outcomes; we could not identify a model specifying the pathways by which SimCoach use would lead to increased help-seeking. The SimCoach team partially adhered to best practices by attempting to use some evidence-based intervention components, such as using screening tools to identify users with PTSD or depression symptoms. However, the tools were adapted for delivery in the SimCoach environment. The PTSD screening tool was not validated against standard PTSD screening tools. The depression screening tool was validated against standard tools but found to be less reliable. Other intervention components, such as the SimCoach Beta recommendations, were not consistently based on the best evidence available. For example, when a participant indicated that he or she was experiencing a symptom of depression or PTSD, SimCoach Beta provided links to websites containing strategies that are not always evidence-based or best practice (e.g., if a user indicated that he or she had trouble concentrating, SimCoach Beta provided a link to a page promoting herbal supplement use, among other strategies, as a remedy). The incorporation of SME expertise is consistent with best practices; however, it is unclear how expert guidance was systematically used to drive the intervention development process. In accordance with best practices for developing complex interventions, SimCoach developers conducted rapid, iterative cycles testing, adapting the design of the content; however, the exploratory trials with users focused only on usability and did not address help-seeking outcomes.

Formative Evaluation of SimCoach Content

One purpose of the formative evaluation was to determine whether SimCoach Beta was acceptable for use in the summative evaluation RCT and to assess any changes necessary to implement the trial. In preparation for requesting approval from the RAND Human Subjects Protection Committee for the RCT, we systematically assessed key components of SimCoach Beta for content that might increase study participant distress or risk.

Overview of SimCoach

SimCoach developers outlined their general approach to intervention development (Rizzo, Gratch, et al., 2009) and gave additional descriptions of methodology in presentations of preliminary results (SimCoach Team in MedVR Group, 2012). They also described a systematic assessment of the SimCoach modality for questionnaire administration (John et al., 2011; Rizzo, Gratch, et al., 2009). For reference, Appendix D includes the original proposal and Appendix E contains the slide deck describing early usability evaluations. SimCoach Beta content consists of screening instruments for PTSD and depression and recommendations that are linked to participant responses.

Approach

We divide our evaluation into three areas: (1) how consistent SimCoach Beta's recommendations to users are with the evidence base, (2) SimCoach Beta's ability to detect user distress, and (3) the validity of the PTSD and depression screening tools that SimCoach Beta administered to users. We compared the personalized recommendations delivered by SimCoach Beta and those provided by VA's National Center for PTSD (National Center for PTSD, undated) and the VA/DoD Depression Clinical Practice Guidelines (Management of Major Depressive Disorder Working Group, 2009). We compared the list of distress phrases that the SimCoach Beta program recognized to trigger referral to crisis hotlines and seven words or word families described by Vannoy and colleagues (Vannoy et al., 2010), which identified 98 percent of suicide discussions from transcripts of discussions between primary care patients and their providers. Finally, we compared the PTSD and depression screening instruments administered by SimCoach Beta and existing screening instruments for these disorders. We describe in the next section how the content of SimCoach Beta compares with these sources of evidence and resources.

Results

Results for the specific evaluation areas are discussed in this section. A general observation about the SimCoach Beta content was that many of the recommendations directed users to self-help resources rather than providing suggestions for seeking help from others.

Consistency of SimCoach-Provided Recommendations with the Evidence Base and Expert Guidance

Several Internet-based interventions have been developed to address traumatic stress and depression-related mental health problems (e.g., van Rosmalen-Nooijens et al., 2013; Mouthaan et al., 2013; Reins et al., 2013; Donkin et al., 2013). Systematic reviews show that several aim to provide self- or therapist-guided treatment, with a few using the provision of feedback aimed at increasing formal help-seeking (Amstadter et al., 2009). A recent systematic review of interventions to increase help-seeking for depression, anxiety, and emotional distress found that interventions that use psychoeducational strategies to increase mental health destigmatize mental illness or provide help-seeking source information improve intentions to seek professional help for mental health problems (Gulliver et al., 2012). However, none has been shown to improve actual help-seeking behavior. Instead, a small literature base seems to suggest that Internet-based interventions that include personalized feedback about symptoms and severity appear to improve help-seeking behavior compared with controls (Christensen et al., 2006; Walters, Miller, and Chiauzzi, 2005).

SimCoach Beta appears to contain elements of several intervention types known to increase help-seeking intentions, including using psychoeducation to increase mental health literacy, destigmatize mental illness, and provide help-seeking source information. Specifically, SimCoach Beta provides information about PTSD and depression symptoms and symptom management (mental health literacy) and communicates that such symptoms are common reactions to trauma (destigmatization). In addition to the psychoeducational elements just described, much of the SimCoach Beta content is focused on providing personalized feedback regarding participants' symptoms, including recommendations for online content and resources for help, suggesting that SimCoach Beta has potential to actually increase help-seeking behavior. We compared the content of the SimCoach Beta feedback and best available evidence for such statements.

Given that the target population for SimCoach is active-duty military service members and veterans or family members of service members or veterans, the most relevant clinical guidelines by which to evaluate SimCoach Beta recommendations are the *VA/DoD Clinical Practice Guidelines: Management of Post-Traumatic Stress Disorder and Acute Stress Reaction* (see VA, 2010) and *VA/DoD Clinical Practice Guideline for the Management of Major Depressive Disorder* (Management of Major Depressive Disorder Working Group, 2009). These guidelines were developed jointly under the auspices of the Veterans Health Administration and DoD to provide evidence-based recommendations that could assist health care providers and patients with decisionmaking in the management of PTSD and major depressive disorder (MDD). The guidelines were developed using a systematic process that involved review of existing guidelines, evaluation of research evidence, and expert consensus when evidence was lacking. Although these guidelines are the most relevant to the SimCoach target population, both sets of guidelines are intended for use within clinical settings rather than in screening and education outside a clinical setting. We were unable to identify any other relevant evidence-based guidelines that address screening and education for depression or PTSD outside of clinical settings (Forbes et al., 2010).

The PTSD guidelines report that there is no specific evidence to guide education about PTSD for people with trauma exposure or with PTSD symptoms. There was expert consensus that trauma survivors should be given information to "normalize common reactions to trauma, improve coping, enhance self-care, facilitate recognition of significant problems, and increase knowledge of and access to services" (VA, 2010). The guidelines suggest that such information could be delivered through a variety of means, including public media. Also based on expert consensus, the guidelines recommend that those people with PTSD should receive additional education about the nature of PTSD symptoms, practical steps to cope with trauma-related problems, and the nature of the recovery process and PTSD treatment.

The VA/DoD depression guidelines also recommend education for people with depression. The guidelines describe evidence to support educational messages about the use of exercise, behavioral activation, and guided self-help for the self-management of depression and fair evidence for educational messages about the nature and course of depression, treatment options, importance of treatment adherence, and relapse prevention strategies.

The SimCoach Beta–provided recommendations (i.e., the educational messages provided in response to endorsement of a symptom) are summarized in Appendix A. The evaluation team found that the SimCoach Beta PTSD recommendations were consistent with the overall spirit of the guideline recommendations to explain PTSD symptoms and provided practical coping strategies; however, the specific content differed significantly from the educational messages provided by the National Center on PTSD. The recommendations directed users to websites containing strategies for alleviating symptoms. The sources of the information on the sites were often unclear, and many of the sites were often not associated with a credible entity (e.g., National Institutes of Health, National Center for PTSD). The sites often supplied multiple strategies for alleviating a symptom, but they did not align with the messaging provided by the National Center for PTSD. For example, the SimCoach Beta–provided recommendations included some links to websites with content not consistent with evidence-based treatment guidelines, such as blogs whose content does not appear to be monitored by professionals.

The SimCoach Beta–provided depression recommendations were consistent with the guideline recommendations about the use of exercise to address depression; however, the recommendations did not reference the other educational messages recommended by the guidelines. In other words, the SimCoach Beta recommendations were incomplete, providing users with only one evidence-based option for managing symptoms of depression. An additional, important shortcoming of SimCoach Beta recommendations was that links to websites discussing non–evidence-based strategies for addressing depression (e.g., herbal remedies) were included, undifferentiated from links to sites describing evidence-based interventions.

Informed by our review of the SimCoach Beta–provided recommendations, we suggested several instances in which the SimCoach team might provide an alternative recommendation based on the *VA/DoD Clinical Practice Guidelines for Depression* (Management of Major Depressive Disorder Working Group, 2009) or the VA National Center for PTSD website (National Center for PTSD, undated). These recommended changes are included in Appendix A and were implemented by the SimCoach team prior to the RCT.

Managing User Distress

SimCoach Beta also contained algorithms to respond to participant distress. If a participant endorsed the PHQ-9 item about having thoughts of self-harm or suicide or if he or she typed words into the chat box that suggest distress, he or she would automatically be routed to a screen with instructions to contact the Veterans Crisis Line. The hotline is staffed 24 hours per day by VA staff trained to manage calls from distressed service members and veterans.

We assessed the list of words (e.g., *suicidal*) developed by the SimCoach team to trigger routing to the screen with instructions to contact the Veterans Crisis Line and provided suggestions for additional distress triggers. These changes were implemented by the SimCoach team prior to the RCT. Vannoy and colleagues (2010) identified seven words or word families used in 98 percent of transcripts of suicide discussions between primary care patients and their providers (*suicid**, *death*, *dying*, *kill**, *hurt**, *harm**, *disappear*). Because the RAND Human Subjects Protection Committee was concerned not only about suicide but also other forms of user distress, our clinical experts added phrases that, according to their clinical expertise, might be likely to capture a wider range of user distress. The complete list of distress triggers is provided in Appendix B.

Validity of Screening Tools

SimCoach Beta used depression and PTSD screening instruments that were adapted versions of the PHQ-9 (Kroenke, Spitzer, and Williams, 2001) and the PCL (Lang et al., 2012) to screen for MDD and PTSD, respectively. The SimCoach team adapted the PHQ-9 and PCL to create its own screening instruments that were aimed to improve user comfort with the virtual human interface (John et al., 2011). The SimCoach team conducted a validation study of the adapted conversational PHQ-9 administered by a virtual human compared with the standard PHQ-9 administered by a human and a virtual human (John et al., 2011). The team found that the standard PHQ-9 had similar reliability whether administered in person or by a virtual human. However, the adapted conversational PHQ-9 used by SimCoach Beta was not found to be reliable and was found to produce significantly higher scores than the other two methods of administration. Users rated the conversational version of the PHQ-9 highly on comfort and ease of use. We are not aware of any studies validating the adapted conversational version of the PCL implemented by the SimCoach team.

Conclusions

We conducted a formative evaluation of the design, development, and pilot implementation of SimCoach Beta. Our assessment indicated that the technical development strategy for SimCoach was well aligned with best practices, and this was consistent with the robust function of the implemented system in both pilot-testing and in the summative evaluation (see Chapter Three). The assessment of the design and development of the SimCoach Beta intervention itself revealed that, although many best practices were observed, there were outstanding issues that could inform future development. Consistently with best practices in intervention development, the development process involved iterative cycles that included measurement of success and adaptations. However, the focus of these assessments was strongly oriented toward improving user experiences interacting with the virtual human characters and not toward help-seeking outcomes. Our evaluation showed that the structured instruments used to measure SimCoach Beta development success during the exploratory trials included limited content related to intentions or barriers to seeking care.

Our review of SimCoach Beta content showed that it included questionnaires, personalized recommendations, and distress triggers. Strengths of the SimCoach Beta content were that it included psychoeducational and destigmatizing interventions shown to increase intentions to seek help, plus symptom-based personalized feedback that (in some cases) has been shown to increase help-seeking behavior. On the other hand, limitations of the content were that the personalized recommendations included directions to self-help resources (e.g., as opposed to professional treatment services) in many cases, a design choice that might affect outcome measures in the RCT related to seeking help from others. Our review of phrases triggering a crisis response was also found to be incomplete, and SimCoach developers made minor modifications to the content of SimCoach Beta to better capture user distress. This included expanding the number and types of phrases that triggered routing participants to crisis hotlines and revising personalized recommendations that were not evidence-based (i.e., herbal remedies). Finally, the adapted conversational version of the PHQ-9 is not comparable to the standard PHQ-9 instrument. The adapted conversational version of the PCL has not been validated like the well-validated standard versions have, so it is unclear whether responses on this instrument are comparable to those on the standard PCL.

CHAPTER THREE

Summative Evaluation

The summative evaluation consisted of an RCT designed to test the efficacy of SimCoach Beta for intermediate, primary outcomes—increasing participant intentions to seek help and decreasing perceptions of stigma associated with seeking care. A secondary goal of the summative evaluation was to evaluate users' experience and engagement with SimCoach Beta—their satisfaction with SimCoach Beta and any distress in using SimCoach Beta compared with the content-matched controls. This component of the study evaluated SimCoach Beta as it was implemented in December 2011. In this chapter, we present the methods and results of the RCT.

Methods

In this section, we discuss our methods for recruitment, screening, design and procedures, data cleaning, and data analysis. All methods were approved by the RAND Human Subjects Protection Committee and received secondary review by DoD.

Recruitment

Participants were service members recruited through the use of Google ads that included keywords related to military service, depression, and PTSD, as well as through advertisements posted on various Facebook groups and online forums of interest to military service members. Before being enrolled in the study, potential participants were screened for eligibility (see "Screening," below). Service members completing the survey were provided with a $25 Amazon.com gift card to compensate them for their time. One key feature of SimCoach not found in traditional referral services is user anonymity. To preserve this feature, we did not collect identifying information from research participants.

Screening

Participants who clicked on a recruitment link were taken to a screen obtaining consent to administer several eligibility screening questions. Participants answered questions about study inclusion criteria (at least 18 years old, being an active-duty or Reserve Component service member or National Guard service member, and being off duty) and exclusion criteria (under the age of 18, being a retired service member or not a service member, being currently on duty, or being incarcerated, on parole, or on probation).

Design and Procedures

Randomization Arms

Once a participant was deemed eligible and had completed an informed-consent form, he or she was randomized to one of the following three conditions:

1. **SimCoach intervention condition:** The participant completed PTSD or depression screening questionnaires using the SimCoach Beta tool, received recommendations, and completed a survey of mental health treatment–seeking intentions.
2. **Content-matched control condition:** The participant completed conventional text-based online PTSD or depression screening questionnaires, received recommendations, and completed a survey of mental health treatment–seeking intentions.
3. **No-treatment control condition:** The participant first completed a survey of mental health treatment–seeking intentions and then chose whether to complete either Sim-Coach Beta or the content-matched intervention.

Regardless of the assigned conditions, each participant was given the choice of answering questions about either PTSD or depression. If the participant did not select either psychological health problem, he or she was randomly assigned to one.

Arm 1: SimCoach Intervention

Participants assigned to the *SimCoach intervention condition* arm interacted with Bill Ford, a simulated human (avatar) enacted in the SimCoach program. Bill Ford is a white male avatar (see Figure 1.1 in Chapter One), representing himself as an Army veteran who spoke with participants in a conversational manner. Participants interacted with Bill Ford by using a chat interface in which they could type responses to him. Bill Ford asked participants a series of questions that corresponded to validated PTSD or depression screening questionnaires. These questions were conversational versions of the six-item version of the PCL (Lang and Stein, 2005) and the PHQ-9 (John et al., 2011), a depression screening inventory (Kroenke, Spitzer, and Williams, 2001). These questions required each participant to report the frequency with which he or she had experienced a variety of PTSD or depression symptoms in the prior month. Frequency was reported on a Likert scale, with response options authored in a conversational tone.

SimCoach Beta then provided personalized recommendations for a symptom if the participant reported experiencing the symptom at one of the two highest frequencies on the response scale. For instance, when Bill Ford asked a participant whether he or she had ever felt distant from somebody, if the participant answered either "Hell yeah. All the time!" or "I sure do. More often than not," that participant received a recommendation. As discussed in Chapter Two, the conversational version of the Patient Health Questionnaire (PHQ) was compared with standard instruments and found to be less reliable (John et al., 2011), but the conversational version of the PCL has not undergone such testing. The provided recommendations consisted of a behavioral recommendation with an accompanying link to a website or online article on the topic. For example, if a participant indicated that he or she was avoiding things that might trigger memories of a traumatic experience, that participant saw a response from Bill Ford indicating that avoidance can be problematic ("It is natural to want to avoid thinking about or feeling emotions about a stressful event. But when avoidance is extreme, or when it's the main way you cope, it can interfere with your emotional recovery and healing. . . .") and a link to the National Center for PTSD web page on avoidance. The full set of recommendations provided in response to each symptom is in Appendix A. After receiving personalized recommendations, each participant moved on to a questionnaire assessing primary and secondary outcomes of treatment-seeking intentions and user experience, respectively (see "Outcome Measures," below).

Arm 2: Content-Matched Control: Conventional Posttraumatic Stress Disorder and Depression Screening Questionnaires

Participants assigned to the content-matched control-condition arm completed text-based versions of the PCL PTSD screening inventory and PHQ-9 depression screening inventory. These instruments used standard, validated language and did not use the modified conversational versions used in the SimCoach intervention condition. As in the SimCoach condition, these questions required each participant to report the frequency with which he or she had experienced a variety of PTSD or depression symptoms. For the PCL, the extent to which respondents experienced each symptom in the prior month is measured on a five-point scale with response options of "not at all," "a little bit," "moderately," "quite a bit," and "extremely." For the PHQ-9, frequency of depression symptoms in the past two weeks was measured on a four-point scale with response options of "not at all," "several days," "more than half the days," and "nearly every day." Again, a participant received recommendations for a symptom if he or she reported having experienced a depression symptom "more than half the days" or "nearly every day" or a PTSD symptom "quite a bit" or "extremely." The same personalized recommendations provided to the SimCoach group were provided as conventional text and links. After receiving personalized recommendations, each participant completed text versions of measures for primary help-seeking, perceived barriers to seeking help, and secondary outcomes (user experience) (see "Outcome Measures," below).

Arm 3: No-Treatment Control

Participants randomly assigned to the no-treatment control-condition arm completed measures of the primary outcome—intentions to seek help—*prior* to being given a choice between SimCoach Beta and the conventional screening administered in the other two arms of the study. After the help-seeking intention questionnaire was administered, each participant was told that he or she would be asked some questions about any PTSD or depression symptoms that he or she might be having and was given the choice between chatting online with a virtual human or using an online form. The virtual-human and online-form options were presented in random order to prevent any influence of ordering on selection of the tool. After either interacting with SimCoach Beta or filling out an online form, the participant completed a questionnaire assessing secondary outcomes (i.e., user experience).

Outcome Measures

Using the SimCoach Beta intervention logic model, we selected standard questionnaires for the primary outcomes of intentions to seek help (Wilson, Deane, and Ciarrochi, 2005) and perceived stigma and barriers to help-seeking among military service members (Britt et al., 2008). We also evaluated secondary outcomes related to user experience and engagement with SimCoach Beta using similar instruments employed by the SimCoach developers.

Primary Study Outcomes

Mental health help-seeking intentions were measured using the General Help Seeking Questionnaire (Wilson, Deane, and Ciarrochi, 2005). Each participant was asked how likely he or she would be to "seek help for issues such as stress, emotional, alcohol, drug, or family problems" from a variety of different sources in the next month. Each participant rated the likelihood of seeking help from a partner, friend, relative, mental health professional, phone help line (e.g., Military OneSource hotline), physician, clergyperson, or someone else. The participant also rated how likely he or she was to "not seek help from anyone." Ratings were made on a seven-point Likert scale (1 = extremely unlikely, 7 = extremely likely). Note that the questionnaire does not assess intentions to seek help from a virtual or online source; however, these intentions could be reflected in the items assessing help from "someone else" and denying a plan to seek help from anyone (reverse scored).

Perceived barriers to seeking help were measured with a questionnaire assessing perceived stigma and barriers to care for psychological problems (Britt et al., 2008). This instrument assesses stigma (six items) and practical barriers that prevent or dissuade people from seeking mental health treatment (five items). Responses could range from *strongly agree* to *strongly disagree*, with mean ratings for the stigma and practical-barriers-to-care items serving as two separate summary scales. Although SimCoach Beta is not likely to affect all items on the scale (e.g., lack of transportation to appointments), we administered the standard instrument to be consistent with other literature.

Secondary Outcomes

Participant choice was used as one measure of user experience and engagement with SimCoach Beta. Each participant assigned to the no-treatment control condition had a choice between SimCoach Beta and the content-matched control conditions (online form). As noted, the order of the choice options (i.e., "use an online form" or "chat with a virtual human") was randomized to avoid order effects.

Participant distress was measured using two questions from the PCL, asking the participant how much he or she experienced repeated, disturbing memories, thoughts, or images of a stressful experience from the past or feeling very upset when something reminded him or her of a stressful experience from the past while using SimCoach or the conventional text screener. Response options were *not at all*, *a little bit*, *moderately*, *quite a bit*, and *extremely*. Any participant responding to either item as *moderately*, *quite a bit*, or *extremely* immediately saw a message encouraging him or her to call 911 or the Veterans Crisis Line if he or she was feeling suicidal. The participant was also asked how he or she felt after using SimCoach or the conventional screening tool compared with how he or she felt before. Ratings were made on a seven-point scale with 1 indicating *much worse than before*, 4 indicating *the same as before*, and 7 indicating *much better than before*.

SimCoach-specific measures were also assessed. Each participant who used SimCoach Beta was asked how much he or she liked using the tool, how interesting he or she found it, how helpful the provided information was, and whether he or she would recommend the tool to others. The participant was also asked how much using the tool increased his or her interest in contacting a professional, as well as how satisfying and comfortable he or she was when using the tool. Finally, each participant rated how much the information provided was relevant to his or her problem, how well he or she understood his or her issue after using the tool, and how effective the tool was in helping him or her plan next steps. The participant rated these items on a scale from 1 to 7, with end points *not at all* and *extremely*. Each SimCoach Beta user also had the opportunity to provide comments about his or her experience using the tool in an open-field response box at the end of the assessment.

Covariates

In the RCT, we collected data on several covariates. Most were administered prior to assignment to experimental condition, with the exception of brief two-item PTSD and PCL symptom assessments, which were administered after the assessment of primary outcomes.

Demographics

To assess the characteristics and representativeness of the population sampled in our study, we asked participants about basic demographics: race and ethnicity, marital status, number of children, gender, and highest level of education obtained.

Branch of Service and Rank

We also assessed branch of service (i.e., Air Force, Army, Marine Corps, or Navy) and rank (pay grade). Early testing of the relationship between user branch of service and rank and user experience may provide insight on how interaction with a SimCoach avatar from the same branch of service may help with development of future versions.

Posttraumatic Stress Disorder and Depression Short Forms

We administered text-based, two-item, short forms for PTSD or depression so that we would have a consistent measure of the participants' mental health. This allowed us to separate participants who are most in need of encouragement to seek help and those who are not.

The two-item PCL screener asked each participant to report the frequency of two PCL items about how much he or she experienced repeated, disturbing memories, thoughts, or images of a stressful experience from the past or feeling very upset when something reminded him or her of a stressful experience from the past in the past month. Each rating was provided on a scale of 1 (*not at all*) to 5 (*extremely*). This screener is both brief and validated as a predictor of PTSD (Lang and Stein, 2005).

To assess current levels of depression, each participant completed the two-item PHQ (PHQ-2) screener, reporting the frequency of two PHQ items about his or her level of interest in doing things and feeling down, each on a scale of 1 (*not at all*), 2 (*few or several days*), 3 (*more than half the days*), and 4 (*nearly every day*). The PHQ-2 screener was included because it is both brief and previously tested (Kroenke, Spitzer, and Williams, 2003).

Data Cleaning

Because of the sensitivity around mental health help-seeking, we purposely opted to preserve anonymity of participants, from recruitment through participation. This introduced risks that some potential participants might provide false answers to screening criteria or attempt to participate in the study multiple times to receive the incentive multiple times. We analyzed the survey metadata to improve the likelihood that analysis data were limited to unique participants attending to the survey content. We eliminated responses from duplicate Internet protocol (IP) addresses, which were stored as one-way encrypted values, and patterns of free-text responses that were associated with those IP addresses. Surveys with response timing between questions that indicated inattention were not analyzed (less than 1 second). This cleaning was conducted independently of and prior to statistical analysis.

Data Analysis

Analysis of the impact that SimCoach Beta use can have on intentions to seek help was based on analyses similar to an intent-to-treat approach. That is, participants were included in analyses under the assumption that they actively engaged with SimCoach Beta and the matched control activities to which they were assigned. The ratings on each of the items in the survey instruments for participants randomized to the SimCoach intervention condition were compared to the content-matched control arm and the no-treatment control arm using pairwise Wilcoxin-Mann-Whitney rank-sum tests, which are robust to nonnormal distributions. Ordered logistic regression, which is also robust to nonnormal distributions, was also used to conduct analyses that allow for the inclusion of covariates (e.g., demographic variables). Though the Wilcoxin-Mann-Whitney rank-sum test and ordered logistic regression compare the rank order of response options across groups (and do not directly compare group means), we opt to report means below to provide a single indicator of how each group responded to each outcome measure. Bonferroni adjustments were applied to confidence-interval (CI) thresholds to reduce the likelihood of detecting false-positive effects for each family of outcomes evaluated.

Each participant completing the survey was administered one of the two intervention modalities: SimCoach Beta or content-matched online forms. (Any participant assigned to the no-treatment control arm was offered a choice between the two options after completing primary outcome measure questionnaires.) Analysis of the user experience questionnaires compared users of SimCoach and those who used the content-matched online forms using a Wilcoxin-Mann-Whitney rank-sum test. Again, Bonferroni adjustments were applied to CI thresholds to reduce likelihood of detecting false positives.

Results

Participant Enrollment

Figure 3.1 shows the retention of participants throughout the recruitment and enrollment process. One thousand three hundred sixty-two potential participants clicked on the screener; 1,029 were excluded based on screening questions, and, of those, 224 surveys were excluded during data cleaning. The survey software randomized a total of 333 people to one of the three arms.

Of the 333 participants randomized to conditions that were not excluded during cleaning, 280 who completed the intervention had complete postintervention survey results. This was the final sample included in the analysis: 109 participants for the SimCoach arm, 68 for the content-matched control arm, and 103 for the no-treatment control arm. Of the 103 in the no-treatment control arm, 79 selected the content-matched online form, and the remaining 24 selected SimCoach Beta. We note that the balance between the three randomization arms was not well-maintained after cleaning, indicating that subjects who were randomized to the content-matched control were more likely to be removed from the analytic sample by data cleaning. Characteristics of the people retained in the final analytic sample are described in the next section.

Participant Characteristics

Participant characteristics are presented in Table 3.1. The population was predominantly white (77.1 percent), male (88.2 percent), and between 25 and 34 years of age (mean age was

Figure 3.1
SimCoach Evaluation Consort Diagram

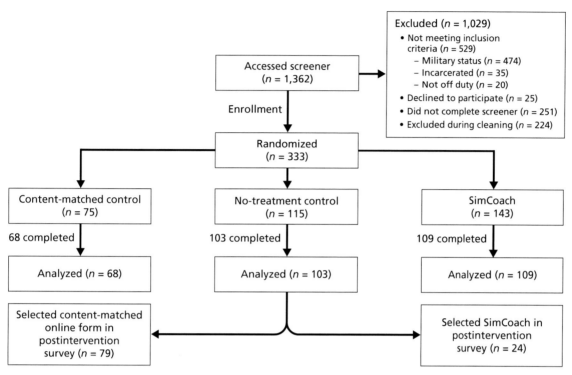

RAND *RR505-3.1*

33.5 years). Participants were distributed across ranks, with most of them concentrated in E4–E9 and O1–O3 statuses. Participants were likely to be married (61 percent).

Participant characteristics generally did not vary across study arms, with the exception of age and marital status; the content-matched control group was older than the other two groups by seven years on average, and members of the SimCoach group were more likely to report that they had never been married.

Primary Outcomes

In this section, we discuss the two primary outcomes of the RCT: help-seeking intentions and perceived barriers to care.

Help-Seeking Intentions

Table 3.2 shows the distribution of responses (ranging from 1, *extremely unlikely*, to 7, *extremely likely*) to the question "How likely is it that you will seek help for issues such as stress, emotional, alcohol, drug, or family problems from the following people in the next month?" across these three groups. The first nine items are indicators of intentions to seek help, while the last ("No one") is a negative indicator, indicating the likelihood that a participant would not seek help. We present the mean score across the first nine items in the final row.

SimCoach condition participants reported significantly greater intentions to seek help from most sources than participants in the content-matched control condition. However, participants in the SimCoach condition did not differ significantly in help-seeking intentions from participants in the no-treatment control condition on any item.

Table 3.1
Participant Characteristics, by Study Arm

Participant Characteristic	No-Treatment Control		SimCoach		Content-Matched Control		All	
	%	95% CI	%	95% CI	%	95% CI	n	%
Gender								
Male	38.1	[32.2–44.3]	38.9	[33.0–45.1]	23.1	[18.2–28.8]	247	88.2
Female	27.3	[14.8–44.8]	39.4	[24.4–56.8]	33.3	[19.4–50.9]	33	11.8
All	36.8	[31.3–42.6]	38.9	[33.4–44.8]	24.3	[19.6–29.7]	280	100.0
Race								
White	39.4	[33.0–46.1]	38.4	[32.1–45.1]	22.2	[17.1–28.3]	216	77.1
Other	28.1	[18.4–40.4]	40.6	[29.3–53.1]	31.2	[21.1–43.6]	64	22.9
All	36.8	[31.3–42.6]	38.9	[33.4–44.8]	24.3	[19.6–29.7]	280	100.0
Age, in years[a]								
18–24	45.9	[30.7–62.0]	40.5	[26.1–56.9]	13.5	[5.7–28.7]	37	13.2
25–34	37.7	[30.1–45.8]	41.8	[34.0–50.0]	20.5	[14.7–27.9]	146	52.1
35–44	37.7	[26.4–50.5]	42.6	[30.8–55.3]	19.7	[11.5–31.6]	61	21.8
45–59	17.4	[6.6–38.4]	26.1	[12.2–47.4]	56.5	[36.2–74.9]	23	8.2
>60	30.8	[12.0–59.2]	7.7	[1.1–39.4]	61.5	[34.2–83.1]	13	4.6
All	36.8	[31.3–42.6]	38.9	[33.4–44.8]	24.3	[19.6–29.7]	280	99.9
Service								
Army	31.7	[24.9–39.3]	41.6	[34.2–49.4]	26.7	[20.4–34.1]	161	57.5
Navy	45	[30.4–60.5]	37.5	[24.0–53.3]	17.5	[8.5–32.5]	40	14.3
Air Force	50	[36.1–63.9]	29.2	[18.0–43.5]	20.8	[11.5–34.7]	48	17.1
Marine Corps	32.3	[18.2–50.4]	41.9	[26.1–59.7]	25.8	[13.4–43.9]	31	11.1
All	36.8	[31.3–42.6]	38.9	[33.4–44.8]	24.3	[19.6–29.7]	280	100.0
Rank								
E1–E3	29.6	[15.5–49.2]	44.4	[27.2–63.2]	25.9	[12.8–45.4]	27	9.6
E4–E6	41.7	[32.6–51.5]	35	[26.3–44.7]	23.3	[16.1–32.5]	103	36.8
E7–E9	36.1	[25.0–48.8]	42.6	[30.8–55.3]	21.3	[12.8–33.4]	61	21.8
O1–O3	33.9	[23.0–46.9]	33.9	[23.0–46.9]	32.2	[21.5–45.1]	59	21.1
O4–O6	36	[19.8–56.1]	44	[26.2–63.5]	20	[8.5–40.1]	25	8.9
O7–O10	25	[3.3–76.5]	75	[23.5–96.7]	0		4	1.4
All	36.9	[31.4–42.8]	38.7	[33.1–44.6]	24.4	[19.7–29.8]	279	99.6
Marital status								

Table 3.1—Continued

Participant Characteristic	No-Treatment Control %	No-Treatment Control 95% CI	SimCoach %	SimCoach 95% CI	Content-Matched Control %	Content-Matched Control 95% CI	All n	All %
Never been married	36.6	[26.2–48.4]	50.7	[39.2–62.2]	12.7	[6.7–22.7]	71	25.4
Living with a partner	23.1	[7.6–52.4]	30.8	[12.0–59.2]	46.2	[22.2–72.0]	13	4.6
Married[a]	38.4	[31.4–45.9]	37.2	[30.3–44.7]	24.4	[18.5–31.4]	172	61.4
Separated	60	[19.9–90.1]	0		40	[9.9–80.1]	5	1.8
Divorced	29.4	[12.7–54.3]	23.5	[9.1–48.7]	47.1	[25.4–69.9]	17	6.1
Widowed	0		50	[5.8–94.2]	50	[5.8–94.2]	2	0.7
All	36.8	[31.3–42.6]	38.9	[33.4–44.8]	24.3	[19.6–29.7]	280	100.0
Endorsed PHQ-2 or PCL-2								
Did not endorse	34	[25.4–43.9]	42	[32.7–51.9]	24	[16.6–33.4]	100	35.7
Endorsed	38.3	[31.5–45.7]	37.2	[30.4–44.6]	24.4	[18.7–31.3]	180	64.3
All	36.8	[31.3–42.6]	38.9	[33.4–44.8]	24.3	[19.6–29.7]	280	100.0

NOTE: PCL-2 = two-item PCL. Because of rounding, some percentage sets do not add up to 100.
[a] Chi-squared test of difference between arms was significant at $p < 0.05$.

Table 3.2
Impact of Intervention on Intention to Seek Help: General Help-Seeking Questionnaire

Likelihood of Seeking Help from This Source	Content-Matched Control	SimCoach	No-Treatment Control
Partner	3.44[a] (1.72)	4.91[a] (1.75)	4.98 (1.63)
Friend	3.32[b] (1.67)	5.07[b] (1.54)	4.87 (1.69)
Parent	3.14[c] (1.81)	4.60[c] (1.73)	4.71 (1.81)
Relative	2.91[d] (1.63)	4.33[d] (1.69)	4.51 (1.82)
Mental health professional	3.97[e] (1.78)	4.78[e] (1.66)	4.91 (1.63)
Phone help line	2.99[f] (1.75)	4.46[f] (1.70)	4.64 (1.69)
Physician	3.33[g] (1.67)	4.49[g] (1.65)	4.59 (1.68)
Ministry	3.13[h] (1.70)	4.33[h] (1.72)	4.33 (1.76)
Someone else	2.83 (1.63)	4.00 (1.98)	3.97 (1.95)
No one	2.95 (1.66)	3.31 (2.11)	3.39 (2.10)
Mean for all nine potential sources of help	3.23 (1.17)	4.55 (1.35)	4.61 (1.33)

NOTE: For comparisons between conditions, means sharing the same letter superscript differ significantly from each other at the $p < 0.01$ level. Responses are on a seven-point Likert scale ranging from *extremely unlikely* (1) to *extremely likely* (7).

To address observed group differences in age and marital status, we also conducted ordered logistic regressions adjusting for demographic factors. The direction, significance, and magnitude of effects were similar to the analyses reported in Table 3.2. To test for different effects among those reporting greater need for help with PTSD and depression-related symptoms, we repeated these analyses in the subgroup of participants that endorsed either the PHQ-2 or PCL-2 items and found no differences in outcomes between participants in the three study conditions (though the study was not designed to have sufficient power to detect subgroup effects).

Perceptions of Stigma Associated with Seeking Help

Because many of the SimCoach utterances were intended to normalize perceived cultural barriers to help-seeking by indicating empathy with users' experiences, and because several recommendations were intended to educate users about efficacious ways to alleviate symptoms, we asked subjects about perceptions of both stigma-related and practical barriers to seeking help. There were no significant differences between study groups in self-reported stigma or practical barriers to care (see Table 3.3).

Table 3.3
Reported Barriers to Help-Seeking

Barrier	Content-Matched Control	SimCoach	No-Treatment Control
I don't trust mental health professionals.	2.62 (1.02)	2.78 (1.10)	3.03 (1.31)
I don't know where to get help.	2.42 (1.12)	2.62 (1.11)	2.89 (1.26)
I don't have adequate transportation.	2.33 (1.25)	2.63 (1.21)	2.67 (1.28)
It is difficult to schedule an appointment.	2.85 (1.13)	2.76 (1.12)	2.82 (1.17)
There would be difficulty getting time off work for treatment.	2.64 (1.25)	2.62 (1.16)	2.84 (1.19)
Mental health care costs too much money.	2.75 (1.26)	2.68 (1.04)	2.83 (1.14)
It would be embarrassing.[a]	2.76 (1.29)	2.89 (1.14)	3.00 (1.06)
It would harm my career.[a]	2.90 (1.00)	2.81 (1.09)	3.11 (1.16)
Members in my unit might have less confidence in me.[a]	2.72 (1.17)	3.02 (1.18)	3.05 (1.16)
My unit leadership might treat me differently.[a]	2.84 (1.20)	2.86 (1.14)	3.07 (1.06)
My leaders would blame me for the problem.[a]	2.67 (1.16)	2.82 (1.18)	2.91 (1.13)
I would be seen as weak.[a]	2.84 (1.19)	2.81 (1.13)	3.18 (1.13)
Mental health care doesn't work.	2.55 (0.93)	2.76 (1.04)	2.82 (1.07)

NOTE: Response options were *strongly disagree, disagree, neither agree nor disagree, agree,* and *strongly agree* (on a 1–5 scale, respectively).
[a] Factors expected to be affected by the SimCoach intervention.

Secondary Outcomes

In this section, we examine secondary outcomes, including the appeal of screening administered by a virtual human versus conventional screening via questionnaire, user experience, and unintended user distress.

Appeal of Virtual Human Versus Conventional Screening

SimCoach developers predicted that a virtual human would be more appealing than more-conventional online tools to encourage help-seeking. To assess this, we examined no-treatment control-group participants' choices between chatting online with a virtual human (i.e., using SimCoach Beta) or using an online form (i.e., completing the same intervention as participants in the content-matched control condition). This hypothesis was not supported. Independently of the order of presentation of the two choice options, 75.9 percent of participants offered the choice elected to use the content-matched control-condition intervention—described as an online form—over engaging with a "virtual human" (SimCoach).

User Experience Outcomes

To help us characterize users' experiences with SimCoach Beta, each participant responded to questions about his or her experience with the tool or the online form, respectively. A total of 133 subjects completed questions about the use of SimCoach Beta, either because they were randomized to the SimCoach condition or because they selected SimCoach Beta use when in the no-treatment control condition. A total of 147 participants were either randomized to or selected the conventional online screener and thus completed questions about the usability of the online form.

As shown in Table 3.4, items assessing satisfaction and comfort with the tool were rated slightly more positively by SimCoach users than by users of the content-matched online form, which is consistent with motivations of SimCoach developers (Rizzo, Buckwalter, et al., 2013). However, it is worth noting that not all participants who completed the satisfaction survey were randomized, which could bias results. SimCoach Beta and online form users did not differ on any of the other user experience measures, such as those assessing the likability of the tool, the helpfulness and relevance of the material, or subsequent interest in contacting a mental health professional.

Comments ranged widely, from highly favorable statements (such as that SimCoach Beta was easier to engage with than clinicians and a good experience) to fears regarding confidentiality and reports of frustration with response speed. A selection of comments from SimCoach Beta users is in Appendix C.

Unintended User Distress

Responses to questions about distress during use of the SimCoach Beta tool are presented in Table 3.5. SimCoach Beta and online form users had low levels of distress during the study. Levels of disturbing memories, thoughts, or images of a stressful experience from the past were not significantly different among SimCoach Beta users and users of the online form. Users in both arms had average responses that suggested that they felt about "the same as before" when compared to how they felt before using the self-assessment tool.

Table 3.4
User Experience Questionnaire

Usability Question	SimCoach (n = 133)	Content-Matched Control (n = 147)
How much did you like using [SimCoach/the self-assessment tool]?	4.68 (1.70)	4.16 (1.72)
How interesting did you find using [SimCoach/the self-assessment tool]?	4.89 (1.20)	4.49 (1.66)
How helpful was the information that you got from using [SimCoach/the self-assessment tool]?	5.06 (1.10)	4.85 (1.51)
How likely would you be to recommend [SimCoach/the self-assessment tool] to other service members?	5.33 (1.33)	4.79 (1.61)
Did using [SimCoach/the self-assessment tool] increase your interest in contacting any professional, like a doctor, a psychologist, or a counselor?	4.54 (1.72)	4.56 (1.70)
How satisfying did you find using [SimCoach/the self-assessment tool]?*	4.99 (1.17)	4.29 (1.53)
How comfortable did you feel providing [SimCoach/the self-assessment tool] information about yourself?*	5.46 (1.21)	4.60 (1.77)
How much was the information that [SimCoach/the self-assessment tool] provided relevant to your problem?	4.72 (1.61)	5.00 (1.37)
How well did you understand your issue after using [SimCoach/the self-assessment tool]?	5.28 (1.12)	5.10 (1.19)
How much was the information that [SimCoach/the self-assessment tool] provided effective in helping you plan your next step?	4.79 (1.64)	4.72 (1.54)

NOTE: All response options were presented on a scale of 1 to 7, with 1 the least favorable and 7 the most favorable value.

* $p < 0.05$ with Bonferroni correction.

Table 3.5
Measures of User Distress

While You Were Using the Tool, Did You Experience These Effects?	SimCoach (n = 133)	Content-Matched Control (n = 147)
Repeated, disturbing memories, thoughts, or images of a stressful experience from the past?[a]	2.34 (1.12)	2.76 (1.16)
Feeling very upset when something reminded you of a stressful experience from the past?[a]	2.60 (1.15)	2.76 (1.33)
Compared to how you felt before using [SimCoach/the self-assessment tool], how do you feel now that you've used it?[b]	4.92 (0.92)	4.57 (0.90)

[a] Response options on a scale of 1 to 5 (*not at all, a little bit, moderately, quite a bit, extremely*).

[b] Response options on a scale of 1 to 7 (1 = *much worse than before*, 4 = *the same as before*, 7 = *much better than before*).

Discussion

We conducted an RCT comparing SimCoach Beta and two control groups: a conventional text-based screening with matched content (online form) and participants in a no-treatment control group. The main finding from this RCT is that intentions to seek help and perceived barriers to seeking help were no greater among SimCoach condition participants than among no-treatment controls. As such, this study did not show that SimCoach Beta resulted in improvements to the two primary outcomes of interest.

However, the version of SimCoach that we evaluated (SimCoach Beta) *was* informed by multiple tests of user experience, and analysis of data relevant to our secondary outcomes of interest—user experience and engagement—indicates that SimCoach Beta users were more satisfied and more comfortable than users of a more conventional text-based screening. This result stands in contrast to the low rate of *selection* of the virtual human for the subjects given the choice between the virtual human and online form modalities, indicating that the way the choice was presented to users could have been modified. In general, neither SimCoach Beta use nor the use of a text-based screening tool resulted in distress for participants. Online form users did not differ on any of the other user experience measures.

Fortunately, SimCoach is a tool that can be constantly improved and adapted. Our evaluation was conducted on a version that had not been informed by any tests of impact on treatment-seeking intentions; evaluations of future versions of SimCoach may find that versions informed by such tests might be more effective.

Limitations

We intentionally designed our study to preserve the anonymity of participants (a key feature of SimCoach) and recruit from a population of service members seeking information online. Despite our efforts to clean participant pools and screen participants, this strategy carries the risk that people may not be sincere or attentive through the questions or may not truly be members of the target population. The results of our findings should be interpreted in light of the paradoxical result that help-seeking intentions were lower for the content-matched control group than they were in the SimCoach or no-treatment control groups. We also assume that SimCoach Beta users actively used SimCoach Beta and that it functioned properly during the trial.

There were some limitations related to the selected measures to assess outcomes, which were selected from among published and validated scales. The General Help Seeking Questionnaire assesses mental health help-seeking but does not assess help-seeking in an online environment—a help-seeking strategy that could be more common among those who choose to access an online screening tool. Also, the instrument we used to assess barriers to care was selected because it was validated and brief and assessed a variety of barriers to care. It does not, however, assess the full range of all possible barriers to care. In the future, a different instrument or modified version of the current instrument could be used to more comprehensively assess barriers.

Finally, the design relied on participant self-report, a strategy that might be better suited to understanding the acceptability and satisfaction with an intervention than the outcomes of that intervention. Because we were able to measure only a proxy of help-seeking behavior (i.e., intention to seek help), we cannot be certain about downstream effects on behavioral outcomes. It might be fruitful to consider longitudinal research designs to allow an assessment of help-seeking behaviors after interaction with these online assessment tools.

CHAPTER FOUR

Summary and Recommendations

In this chapter, we summarize our key findings from both the formative and summative evaluations. We then offer recommendations to both DCoE and the SimCoach developers based on our evaluation results.

Key Findings

Results of the *formative evaluation* indicate the following:

- The SimCoach software system has been developed in alignment with DoD best practices for software development and, in many ways, goes beyond minimum standards. It is, therefore, flexible and adaptable and has extensive potential for technical improvements and alternative applications in collaborative projects.
- The SimCoach Beta intervention development process had mixed alignment with best practices for developing clinical interventions. More could be done to align its ongoing development with existing theory of health behavior or mental health treatment-seeking. Some of the specific content in SimCoach Beta, including the personalized recommendations and distress-management triggers, required modest revision to satisfy human subject protection concerns. In particular, recommended resources and specific behavioral recommendations to users could be further aligned with evidence.
- The depression and PTSD screening instruments employed by SimCoach Beta have been adapted into a conversational style with the aim of improving the user experience; however, they have not been sufficiently validated against the standard PHQ-9 and PCL screening instruments.
- Overall, SimCoach Beta development was heavily focused on user experience with the virtual human rather than on the impact of SimCoach Beta as an intervention intended to improve help-seeking intentions and reduce barriers to seeking help.

Results of the *summative evaluation* indicate the following:

- In an RCT powered to detect a clinically relevant effect size, data showed no significant difference between participants exposed to SimCoach Beta and those not exposed to any intervention intended to modify intentions or attitudes toward seeking help for psychological health.

- Following the intervention, SimCoach Beta users did not vary from the control-group participants in perceptions of stigma associated with help-seeking for symptoms of depression or PTSD.
- When given the choice, fewer participants chose to use SimCoach Beta than chose traditional form-based assessments of PTSD and depression. Confusion or lack of clarity around each of these options, however, may have affected participants' willingness to try SimCoach Beta.
- When participants were either randomly assigned to use SimCoach Beta, or they selected SimCoach Beta by choice over text-based versions of the same content, participants reported greater comfort disclosing symptoms and a more positive user experience than users of the conventional text-based, online forms did.
- Using SimCoach Beta did not result in unintended distress for participants.

Recommendations

We evaluated a version of SimCoach (SimCoach Beta) that was intended to be improved upon and extended. As such, we separate this section into recommendations for the SimCoach developers and recommendations for DCoE, which provided the funds for SimCoach development.

Recommendations for SimCoach Developers

- **Implement best practices in development of help-seeking intervention.** Emerging research suggests specific interventions that may promote service-member help-seeking intentions and behavior. SimCoach developers could consider redesigning components of the intervention to make them more consistent with evidence-based approaches to enhancing help-seeking outcomes overall, and specific to the military population (Bayir and Kagan, 2008; Green, 2000).
- **Consider new approaches to SimCoach marketing.** SimCoach developers anticipated that the novelty of the SimCoach tool would be attractive to potential users. Our findings suggested that advertising SimCoach with only the expression "virtual human" was not sufficient to attract users to select SimCoach over other, more-traditional (online form) options. Once users were exposed to the avatar, however, they were significantly more likely to find it more satisfying than the online form. More-explicit marketing of SimCoach's novel features (for example, including digital images of the avatar and links to sample video) could make SimCoach more attractive to a broader pool of potential users.
- **Use validated screening instruments when possible.** The goal of SimCoach is to identify users at risk for PTSD and depression and provide resources. To do this appropriately, instruments must be sufficiently reliable and have adequate sensitivity (i.e., an ability to properly identify people with the disorder) and specificity (i.e., the ability to properly identify people who do not have the disorder) (Lalkhen and McCluskey, 2008). Because many such instruments are currently available, SimCoach developers may consider including established screening instruments in the program.
- **Consider using an outcome-oriented, iterative development process during subsequent improvements to the SimCoach intervention.** To ensure that the SimCoach intervention is not only appealing to users but also effective in promoting help-seeking,

the development team might identify a small set of outcome-oriented metrics (e.g., in collaboration with SMEs) to be monitored throughout the development process. During early stages of development, these metrics might be based on ratings from the SME team (that might also include members of the target user community). Then, during later stages of development, these metrics could come directly from user evaluations.

- **Continue to design new dialogue and content to meet SimCoach goals of reaching a target audience of service members, veterans, and family members.** The SimCoach team identifies reaching service members, veterans, and family members as a goal. However, the dialogue and resources provided are targeted for service members and veterans only. SimCoach developers may consider the development of new dialogue and content to address the specific needs of military family members and to potentially enhance their engagement with and use of SimCoach.

- **If future versions are found to be effective, develop versions of SimCoach that are compatible with mobile devices and web browsers.** SimCoach Beta is a web-based tool, but, because it uses a Flash® interface, it is not compatible for use with many mobile devices. Given the prevalence of mobile devices, SimCoach developers could consider creating a version of the software that is compatible with mobile devices. In addition, systematic testing of SimCoach functionality with different web browsers and possibly devices, such as screen readers, that allow people with visual disabilities to access websites may enable more people using a variety of technical devices to access the tool.

- **Consider using SimCoach in other cases in which potentially sensitive questionnaires and information may be delivered.** Our evaluation demonstrated that SimCoach Beta users were more comfortable and experienced less distress with the questionnaires and recommendations than users who filled out traditional online forms. Regardless of whether results are intended to encourage help-seeking or other behavioral outcomes, SimCoach could be applied in other circumstances in which potentially sensitive questionnaires and recommendations are necessary. Rigorous empirical evaluation of novel SimCoach applications is needed to demonstrate its utility in other groups or topic areas.

Recommendations for the Defense Centers of Excellence for Psychological Health and Traumatic Brain Injury

Our results do not show any conclusive evidence of the efficacy of SimCoach Beta. In that light, we offer the following recommendations to guide further decisions about DCoE's involvement with SimCoach and similar programs:

- **Consider changing funding models to motivate best practices in intervention development.** To ensure that DCoE invests its development funds in the most-promising technology-based projects, it may wish to require submission of pilot data prior to the funding of a large project. This approach is consistent with emerging federal funding models from the National Institutes of Health, such as the UH2/UH3 grant mechanisms that provide continuation funding for large projects contingent on clearly stated results of a pilot year. DCoE may also explore the benefit of having proposed interventions be theory-based and that instruments be validated, where possible.

- **Support pilot evaluations and dissemination approaches in different contexts.** Some of our results call into question an original premise of SimCoach—that it will be more attractive and engaging to users than conventional interventions. Although this was true when comparing user experiences postintervention, about three-quarters of users who were offered the choice between a "virtual human" and an "online form" without seeing SimCoach selected more-conventional online forms. Supporting pilot evaluation and dissemination efforts that place SimCoach in more-interactive environments might help DCoE identify high-value placement of SimCoach.

- **Consider investing in strategies to guide the development of technology-based clinical interventions.** We were unable to identify well-developed best practices for developing technology-based interventions intended to affect clinical or behavioral outcomes. If DCoE anticipates overseeing the development of multiple technology-based programs, DCoE (perhaps in partnership with other relevant agencies) might consider convening domain experts from clinical psychology, the user experience community, and the artificial intelligence and VR community to create such guidance to inform future work. Alternatively, DCoE may express this need to other agencies with more-extensive expertise in technology-based intervention development to spur efficient work in this regard.

- **DCoE might play an active role in design and monitoring of outcome-oriented progress metrics for technology development projects.** Our evaluation shows that SimCoach developers have excellent foundations and motivation to create best-in-class virtual humans and flexible software design. However, the *application* of this technology to the use case of improving help-seeking intentions has not yet reached full potential. If adherence to outcome-oriented objectives is a priority for DCoE resource allocation, DCoE may consider building ongoing process and outcome monitoring into its future intervention development contracts, akin to a continuous quality improvement approach.

Conclusions

Technology-driven interventions, such as SimCoach, are on the forefront of clinical psychology, and there is no established set of best practices that marries software development and development of clinical interventions. Although SimCoach had a strong approach to software engineering, and although the results of the RCT suggest that users had satisfactory experiences using this version of SimCoach (SimCoach Beta), participants did not show greater intentions to seek help than users who did not receive any questionnaires or recommendations. It is possible that an outcome-oriented approach to developing software for behavioral change over a user experience–oriented approach might be preferable in this particular domain of interventions. Stakeholders in SimCoach and other technology-driven behavioral interventions might consider coordinating a consensus process for creating best practices and principles for future reference.

Revisions to SimCoach Beta Recommendations

Recommendations for Those Reporting Posttraumatic Stress Disorder Symptoms

The SimCoach team implemented rules to determine which recommendations were supplied to respondents endorsing PTSD symptoms on the PCL screening tool (Lang and Stein, 2005). A participant was considered to exhibit a symptom if he or she chose one of two affirmative responses (e.g., for a question asking about the frequency of flashbacks, responding with "that happens to me fairly often" or "yeah, I get that all the time") or if he or she answered three or more questions to the second-lowest degree (e.g., for the flashbacks question, answering "I had that happen a couple of times"). If a participant reported zero symptoms, that participant did not receive any recommendations. If a participant demonstrated one or more symptoms, Sim-Coach Beta repeated the symptoms, then showed the following text:

> Off the bat, there's a couple of things that you should keep in mind. Try to find someone to talk to about this stuff, read more about this thing you're going through, and try getting back into the swing of things.

SimCoach Beta then asked whether the participant was comfortable with diving a little deeper. If the participant responded affirmatively, SimCoach Beta provided a recommendation.

Table A.1 lists the PTSD symptom that could be endorsed, the conversational wording implemented in SimCoach Beta, the original recommendation suggested by SimCoach Beta, and the revised recommendation implemented after evaluation by our team. The recommendations supplied by our team are based on information available at the National Center for PTSD (National Center for PTSD, undated).

Recommendations for Those Reporting Depressive Symptoms

The SimCoach team implemented rules to determine which recommendations were supplied to respondents endorsing depression symptoms on the PHQ screening tool (Kroenke, Spitzer, and Williams, 2001). A participant was considered to exhibit a symptom if he or she chose one of two affirmative responses (e.g., for question on appetite, responding with "not great" or "no") or if they answered three or more questions to the second-lowest degree (e.g., for the appetite question, answering "mostly"). As with the PTSD module, if a participant endorsed

Table A.1
SimCoach Beta–Provided Recommendations for Coaching for Posttraumatic Stress Disorder Symptoms

PTSD Symptom	SimCoach Language for Asking About Symptom	Original SimCoach Beta Recommendation Provided	Revised Recommendation (based on National Center for PTSD recommendations)
Feeling distant	You said that [subject: you, he, she] [~subject:'ve,'s,'s] been feeling distant lately. [~subject: You, He, She] ever talk to somebody else who's been feeling that way?	Talking to somebody who's feeling the same way, might help [pron: you, him, her] start to sort through [~pron: your, his, her] own feelings. Trauma survivors with PTSD may have trouble with their close family relationships or friendships. The symptoms of PTSD can cause problems with trust, closeness, communication, and problem solving. These problems may affect the way the survivor acts with others. In turn, the way a loved one responds to him or her affects the trauma survivor. A circular pattern can develop that may sometimes harm relationships. http://www.ptsd.va.gov/public/pages/ptsd-and-relationships.asp [National Center for PTSD, 2014]	No new recommendation suggested because the suggested resource links to the National Center for PTSD.
Feeling irritable	You said that [subject: you, he, she] is feeling irritable. [~subject: You, He, She] ever tried controlling it?	This article might help with that, it's an interesting idea. Trauma makes some people feel powerless. PTSD makes you feel powerless. I read an article today, it lists causes of PTSD as the usual life-threatening events plus: extreme feelings of powerlessness. . . . http://healmyptsd.com/2009/08/treating-ptsd-taking-control-of-the-picture.html [Rosenthal, 2009]	Replace the URL with the following: http://www.ptsd.va.gov/public/pages/anger-and-trauma.asp
Having flashbacks	You mentioned having flashbacks. [subject: You, He, She] ever connect with somebody else who's been having that same problem?	It's more common than you might think. Memories, Flashbacks and Dissociation as a Function of Combat PTSD/TBI: Experiential Research http://ptsdasoldiersperspective.blogspot.com/2011/06/memories-flashbacks-and-dissociation-as.html [Lee, 2011]	Replace the URL with the following: http://ptsd.about.com/od/selfhelp/a/flashcoping
Getting upset at memories	Okay, you said [subject: you, he, she] [~subject:'ve,'s,'s] been getting upset lately. [~subject: You, He, She] ever thought about how to control that?	It helps, airing out that stuff. Like a room that's been kept shut too long—it hurts when that door opens, but it's good. Resource: Coping with Flashbacks http://ptsd.about.com/od/selfhelp/a/flashcoping.htm [Tull, 2014]	No recommendation provided.
Avoiding things that might trigger memories	Avoidance might feel good now, but it's not helping [pron: you, him, her] in the long run.	Avoidance is a common reaction to trauma. It is natural to want to avoid thinking about or feeling emotions about a stressful event. But when avoidance is extreme, or when it's the main way you cope, it can interfere with your emotional recovery and healing. . . . http://www.ptsd.va.gov/public/pages/avoidance.asp [National Center for PTSD, date unknown]	No new recommendation suggested because the suggested resource links to the National Center for PTSD.

NOTE: Because of the dynamic nature of the Internet, some web addresses shown might no longer work.

no symptoms, no recommendations were provided. For a participant endorsing one or more symptoms, SimCoach Beta repeated the symptoms, then showed the following text:

> Off the bat, there's a couple of things that you should keep in mind. Try to find someone to talk to about this stuff, read more about this thing you're going through, and try getting back into the swing of things.

SimCoach Beta then asked the participant whether he or she was comfortable with diving a little deeper. If the participant indicated that he or she was, SimCoach Beta provided a recommendation.

Table A.2 lists the depression symptom that could be endorsed, the conversational wording implemented in SimCoach Beta, the original recommendation suggested by SimCoach Beta, and the revised recommendation implemented after evaluation by our team. For the purposes of the RCT, the evaluation team reviewed the SimCoach Beta recommendations and made some revisions based on concerns that some of the recommended links suggested strategies that were not evidence-based (for example, suggesting herbal remedies). However, to ensure that the RCT was testing a version of SimCoach Beta that was close to what was designed by the SimCoach team, the evaluation team attempted to make only changes needed to ensure participant safety.

Table A.2
SimCoach Beta–Provided Recommendations for Coaching for Depressive Symptoms

Depression Symptom	SimCoach Language for Asking About Symptom	Original SimCoach Beta Recommendation Provided	Revised Recommendations Based on VA/DoD Clinical Practice Guidelines for Depression
Not doing a lot of things that make [pron: you, him, her] happy	Okay, you said [subject: you, he, she] [~subject: haven't, hasn't, hasn't] been feeling so happy lately. There could be a lot of reasons for that. But first off, [~subject: have, has, has] [~subject: you, he, she] done any exercise recently?	Well, it might be worth a try. Gettin' some exercise has been medically proven to lift people's spirits. http://www.time.com/time/health/article/0,8599,1998021,00.html [Blue, 2010]	Replace the URL with the following: http://www.ptsd.va.gov/public/pages/coping-ptsd-lifestyle-changes.asp
Kind of low energy	Okay, you said [subject: you, he, she] [~subject: haven't, hasn't, hasn't] had much energy lately. There's about a million possible explanations for that, from how [~subject: you, he, she] [~subject:'ve,'s,'s] been sleeping, to what [~subject: you, he, she] [~subject:'ve,'s,'s] been eating, to things like job stress. You have an idea of what it might be?	Well, maybe take a look at this list of suggestions about how to fight tiredness, and see if anything clicks. Fatigue can mean feeling tired, lethargic, sleepy or lacking energy. Tips to fight fatigue include drinking lots of water, limiting caffeine, improving your diet, and getting enough sleep. Activity and physical exercise help fight fatigue. Fatigue can have a medical cause, so check with your doctor. Fatigue can also be a symptom of stress, anxiety, grief, or depression. http://www.betterhealth.vic.gov.au/bhcv2/bhcarticles.nsf/pages/Fatigue_fighting_tips [State Government of Victoria, 2011]	No recommendation provided.

Table A.2—Continued

Depression Symptom	SimCoach Language for Asking About Symptom	Original SimCoach Beta Recommendation Provided	Revised Recommendations Based on VA/DoD Clinical Practice Guidelines for Depression
Feelin' fidgety or sluggish	Okay, you said [subject: you, he, she] [~subject:'ve,'s,'s] either been feeling real fidgety lately, or real sluggish. You ever thought about [~subject: your, his, her] diet?	There's probably more at work than just food, but there's a pretty big connection between what we eat and how we feel, energy-wise. This article might give you some ideas about what to eat to feel differently. Every day, millions of people complain about being tired, and it is really no wonder, what with the amount of things that we all need to get done in a day. There are so many things to do and so little time to get them done, and we all wish that there were at least 25 hours in a day. Most people want to find a way to get more energy and not feel so tired but are not sure of what they can do about it. . . . http://healthy-lifestyle.most-effective-solution.com/2008/01/10/tips-to-boost-energy-and-stop-feeling-tired/ [Borzack, 2008]	Replace the URL with the following: http://www.nlm.nih.gov/medlineplus/ency/article/003088.htm ["Fatigue," 2013].
Not sleeping great	Okay, you said [subject: you, he, she] [~subject:'ve,'s,'s] been having some trouble sleeping, so let's take a look at that. You ever heard of sleep hygiene?	It's your basic good sleeping habits. Good "hygiene" is anything that helps you to have a healthy life. The idea behind sleep hygiene is the same as dental hygiene. Dental hygiene helps you stay healthy by keeping your teeth and gums clean and strong. Sleep hygiene helps you stay healthy by keeping your mind and body rested and strong. Following these tips will help you sleep better and feel your best. http://www.sleepeducation.com/Hygiene.aspx [American Academy of Sleep Medicine, undated]	No recommendation provided.
Not concentrating so well	Okay, you said [subject: you, he, she] [~subject:'ve,'s,'s] been having some trouble concentrating, so let's take a look at that. There could be a lot of reasons for this. Could be related to [~subject: your, his, her] body, like not having enough sleep, or could be more mental, like having a lot of stress. Or hell, maybe [~subject: your, his, her] neighbor's car alarm goes off every fifteen minutes!	6 Simple Ways to Boost Concentration (Article): Poor concentration is something that we all suffer from time to time, but there is no need to worry. There are some great natural remedies and tricks available to help boost your concentration and memory, including the six simple ways outlined below. . . . http://www.naturaltherapypages.com.au/article/Poor_Concentration ["6 Simple Ways to Boost Concentration," 2008]	Replace with the following text and URL: You can find some tips for boosting your concentration in the "Difficulty concentrating or staying focused" section on this website: http://www.ptsd.va.gov/public/pages/coping-traumatic-stress.asp

Table A.2—Continued

Depression Symptom	SimCoach Language for Asking About Symptom	Original SimCoach Beta Recommendation Provided	Revised Recommendations Based on VA/DoD Clinical Practice Guidelines for Depression
Not eating regularly	Okay, you said [subject: you, he, she] [~subject:'ve,'s,'s] been having some trouble with [~subject: your, his, her] appetite. Granted, I'm not [a] nutrition coach, or whatever they call them, but seems like if [~subject: your, his, her] appetite's off it's probably a sign something else is wrong. Would you say this problem is new?	Well, when my computer crashed, the first thing the tech asked me was if I'd installed any new software recently. So I'm thinking this change in appetite probably has something to do with some other big change in your life. The bottom line, to me anyway, is that if it's affecting your health, you should definitely see a doctor.	No recommendation provided.
Feeling depressed	Okay, you said [subject: you, he, she] [~subject: haven't, hasn't, hasn't] been feeling so happy lately. There could be a lot of reasons for that. But first off, [~subject: have, has, has] [~subject: you, he, she] done any exercise recently?	Well, it might be worth a try. Gettin' some exercise has been medically proven to lift people's spirits. http://www.time.com/time/health/article/0,8599,1998021,00.html [Blue, 2010]	Replace the URL with the following: http://www.ptsd.va.gov/public/pages/depression-and-trauma.asp
Feeling bad about [pron: you, him, her] [~pron: rself, self, self]	Okay, you said [subject: you, he, she] [~subject: haven't, hasn't, hasn't] been feeling bad about [~subject: yourself, himself, herself], like [~subject: you, he, she] let someone down or screwed something up. [~subject: have, has, has] [~subject: you, he, she] ever written down [~subject: your, his, her] thoughts about this?	Well, I think it's probably a good idea. When one keeps things bottled up inside one's head they just swirl around and around in there. Writing it down always makes me feel a bit of relief. Doesn't have to be a fancy poem or anything, just something to get your thoughts down on paper.	Replace text with the following: http://www.ptsd.va.gov/public/pages/depression-and-trauma.asp

Table A.2—Continued

Depression Symptom	SimCoach Language for Asking About Symptom	Original SimCoach Beta Recommendation Provided	Revised Recommendations Based on VA/DoD Clinical Practice Guidelines for Depression
Thinking about hurting [pron: you, him, her] [~pron: rself, self, self]	Okay, you said [subject: you, he, she] [~subject:'ve,'s,'s] been thinking about hurting [~subject: yourself, himself, herself] in some way. I gotta tell you, I'm just not equipped to handle that kind of thing. If [~subject: you're, he's, she's] having thoughts of suicide, you need to call 911 right now. If [~subject: you're, he's, she's] not in the US, find [~subject: your, the, the] local emergency number and dial it. Make sure you stay on the phone with the operator and wait for help to arrive. People out there care about what happens to [~subject: you, him, her]. [~subject: Your, His, Her] life is extremely valuable. Just dial the number—people are waiting to help [~subject: you, him, her].	No further resource given.	No recommendation given. An affirmative response triggers the distress protocol described elsewhere in this report.

NOTE: Because of the dynamic nature of the Internet, some web addresses shown might no longer work.

Additional Distress Signal Phrases

Vannoy and colleagues (2010) have the following list of distress-signal phrases:

- suicid*
- hurt*
- death
- harm*
- dying
- disappear
- kill*.

The asterisk indicates a wild card in that any text string with the characters preceding the asterisk would match; for example, *suicid** matches *suicide* or *suicidal*.

Our clinical experts provided some additional distress-signal phrases:

- hate
- dead
- end it all
- worthless
- hopeless
- nothing will ever change
- hurt
- overdose
- pissed off
- cut
- slit
- shoot
- lose it
- strangle
- hang
- revenge
- take my [or his or her or their] life
- hit
- rage
- out of control
- bleed

- agitated
- feel* trapped
- die
- no hope
- no reason to live
- gun
- end my [or his or her or their] life
- no purpose
- knife
- what's the point?
- can't take it anymore
- commit
- why am I here?
- crash.

SimCoach Beta Participant Comments

We include here some of the free-text comments received from SimCoach Beta users in the survey. There were several favorable comments indicating that the information presented was useful or relevant but that it might be better tailored to the particular circumstances and experiences of the user. One user expressed confidentiality concerns, and another directly commented on what appeared to be technical difficulty. Other comments were not so much directly related to SimCoach Beta use as to the overall barriers service members face in seeking psychological health care:

- "Sometimes there wasn't a long enough break in the question to response time and it caused it to say that your answer was [irrelevant] because it was like you answered the second question he asked, when you just only submitted the answer for the first."
- "Maybe it was due to my doing this in my home and did not have to look in the doc face that made it easier for me to admit that I have issues as I have always known; something was wrong but did not know what to do."
- "One of your PTSD questions about feeling you were in danger was too specific in that it seemed to cater to an infantryman patrolling in a combat zone. I was an Aviator flying in a combat zone. There was a constant threat to being engaged by the enemy. Depending on which Forward Operating Base (FOB) the Soldiers resided, there were also continuous and/or frequent mortar attacks that posed a danger. Fortunately for my Unit, the enemy was rarely accurate with its mortars, but the odd chance was always present that they could get lucky and put a mortar in the Unit area."
- "Am still in the service. Have had inpatient treatment for trauma with VA, still attempting to get help and get through each day."
- "I am just not sure this is confidential & that no one will find out."
- "The biggest thing is that leadership has to not only SAY that seeking help is a sign of strength and when done appropriately will not harm your career but also SHOW by their ACTIONS that this is true."
- "This survey is great for those who are unsure if they have PTSD/Depression. For those like myself who have been getting treated for some time, it is more of just a refresher. But at the same time I see it as a good thing that places like this are here getting information about those who may have it, and providing some information about it at the same time."
- "SimCoach repeated the same question three times, and I don't feel it provided me any new information."
- "Thanks, this is a very interesting experience."

SimCoach Proposal

This appendix contains the original proposal for the development of SimCoach, which the SimCoach development team provided to the authors at the beginning of the evaluation.

SimCoach: Promoting Healthcare Outreach and Advocacy with Virtual Humans

Contract Number: W911NF-04-D-0005
Task Number:

Technical Points of Contact:

Skip Rizzo
University of Southern California
Institute for Creative Technologies
13274 Fiji Way, Marina del Rey, CA 90292
(310) 301-5018
rizzo@ict.usc.edu

Jon Gratch
University of Southern California
Institute for Creative Technologies
13274 Fiji Way, Marina del Rey, CA 90292
(310) 448-0306
gratch@ict.usc.edu

Julia Kim
University of Southern California
Institute for Creative Technologies
13274 Fiji Way, Marina del Rey, CA 90292
(310) 301-5012
kim@ict.usc.edu

Stacy Marsella
University of Southern California
Institute for Creative Technologies
13274 Fiji Way, Marina del Rey, CA 90292
(310) 448-0369
marsella@ict.usc.edu

Administrative Point of Contact:
Caron Thomas, Senior Contract and Grant Administrator
University of Southern California
Department of Contracts and Grants
837 W. Downey Way, Room 330
Los Angeles, CA 90089-1147
(213)740-6478 (V), (213) 740-6070 (F)
chthomas@ooc.usc.edu

Period of Performance:
September 1, 2009 – August 31, 2011

Table of Contents

Executive Summary

This effort is being performed under the Institute for Creative Technologies (ICT) contract being managed by the United States Army Research, Development and Engineering Command (RDECOM) Simulation and Training Technology Center (STTC). The mission of the Institute for Creative Technologies is to build a partnership among the entertainment industry, Army, and academia with the goal of creating synthetic experiences so compelling, that participants react as if they are real. The result is engaging new immersive technologies for learning, training, and operational environments.

Within the military population (which includes both warfighters and warfighter families), the need for healthcare information is growing at an astounding rate. In spite of a Herculean effort on the part of the DOD to produce and disseminate behavioral health programs for military personnel and their families, the complexity of the issues involved continue to challenge the best efforts of military mental health care experts, administrators and providers. Since 2004, numerous blue ribbon panels of experts have attempted to assess the current DOD and VA healthcare delivery system and provide recommendations for improvement. Most of these reports cite a need for identification and implementation of ways to enhance the healthcare dissemination/delivery system for military personnel and their families in a fashion that provides better awareness and access to care while reducing the stigma of help-seeking. In essence, new methods are required to reduce barriers to care.

To address such barriers, the University of Southern California (USC) Institute for Creative Technologies (ICT) proposes to develop and deliver an intelligent, interactive program referred to as SimCoach. The SimCoach experience will be designed to **attract** and **engage** Warfighters and their significant others who might not otherwise seek help (whether due to stigma, lack of awareness or a general reluctance to seek help). **The goal will be to create an experience that will motivate these Warfighters and their significant others to take the first step – to empower themselves with regard to their healthcare** (e.g., psychological health and traumatic brain injury) **and general personal welfare** (i.e., other non-medical stressors such as economic or relationship issues) – and encourage them to take the next step towards seeking other, more formal resources that are available. SimCoach will not be able to breakdown all the barriers identified above or provide diagnostic or therapy services. Rather, SimCoach will aim to foster comfort and confidence in promoting users' effort to understand their situation better, explore available options and initiate the treatment process when needed.

SimCoach will be a part of a holistic experience designed to attract, engage, and empower the users. Users will ideally be able to access the system with a low-end computer and no special software (the desired platform is the web, but technical feasibility will need to be assessed to determine if the entire experience – especially the virtual humans – can be delivered through the web). The users will also be allowed to remain completely anonymous. When they arrive, the users will find a very simple launch point that will allow them to explore specific psychological health and TBI-related issues if they are already self-directed or to "wander around" to get

3

comfortable with the system and/or the issues that they may (or may not) be facing. The user will likely be able to use the site without having to create a user account, but, if they wish to have some persistence, they will have the ability to create an account – though this account will also be totally anonymous if they so desire.

SimCoach will provide users with a choice of options for selecting from a variety of virtual human characters and personalities. Some may not give advice at all. They may serve only to encourage or perhaps take more of a Socratic and/or Eliza approach, asking many questions that encourage the user to generate their own ideas. Others may be very fact- and information-based. For example, experts on specific clinical topics may convey healthcare information in an accurate and accessible fashion that does not come off as condescending. Some characters could be based on specific interests of the users – such as a virtual Tiger Woods that appeals to golfers who can find out more about how to use golf as a part of a medical or personal regimen. Other characters could be embodied as clinical military personnel, armed with first hand knowledge that is perceived by the user to be more relevant to their experience. Chaplain characters could also be created for those who would be more trusting of a coach that can present helpful content from a more spiritual background. Input from the clinical team and output of early focus groups will serve to prioritize which classes of characters will be deployed for the initial implementation.

Based on information garnered through the interaction between the user and the virtual human, as well as the evocative design of the specific avatar, the user will be given appropriate levels of direct or indirect information or suggestions regarding access to relevant information on psychology, social work, neurology, rehabilitation, the military healthcare system, and also to other Service Members. Healthcare information that users will be directed to for this project will come primarily from the DCoE's six affiliated center sites related to these issues -- Defense and Veterans Brain Injury Center, Center for Deployment Psychology, Deployment Health Clinical Center, Center for the Study of Traumatic Stress, National Intrepid Center of Excellence, and the National Center for Telehealth & Technology, in addition to such related sites as *After Deployment*, *Battlemind* and the *National Center for PTSD*. Users will also be directed to experts on specific topics including stress, depression, brain injury, relationship counseling, substance abuse, suicide, rehabilitation, reintegration and other relevant specialties as appropriate. In addition to interaction with avatars, the system will deliver complementary content that will augment the interactions with the characters. This could include edited content such as articles, video testimonials and blog posts as well as connection to peers and other support systems through forums and community groups. There will also be options to allow the user to perform some simple neurocognitive and psychological tests to help inform self-awareness or aid in making decisions on initial referral options. Users will also have the option to print out a summary of the computerized sessions to bring with them when seeking medical treatment to enhance their comfort level, armed with knowledge, when dealing with human clinical care providers and experts.

The system will allow users to flexibly interact with this character by typing text, clicking on character generated menu options and, potentially, limited speech interaction during the initial phases of development. The specific interaction methods will be developed as a part of a design effort based on a deep exploration of the user base and their needs. We will explore the feasibility of supporting as much natural language (typed and spoken) as possible – with short-term decisions made based on technical feasibility, risk mitigation, and the need to demonstrate capabilities even if they are not fully mature.

The software principle underlying the design of SimCoach is to create a backbone that can grow organically over time and does not tie the government to a single developer. We will design the software to be open, modular, and easy to extend and author content. Where possible, the system will incorporate open source modules and open standards to facilitate incorporation in a modular fashion to facilitate incorporation of the latest advances in language processing, graphics, artificial intelligence, and other technological requirements. A series of content development tools will facilitate the creation of new virtual human characters by non-technical clinicians so that the system can grow and expand over time with new experts and focus areas as required.

The goal of the SimCoach experience will be to attract and engage warfighters and significant others who might not otherwise seek help. A fundamental challenge of this project is to better understand this user base and their attitudes such that appropriate user experiences can be designed that will reduce barriers to help-seeking and care. This population is likely to be a diverse group of individuals with a myriad of needs. Among the things that the system will likely have to do is break down mistrust, be helpful for the user whether the user trusts the system, and keep the user coming back for continued assistance as needed or until the user decides to seek assistance from a recommended care provider.

The proposed work effort is covered in the ICT Basic Contract Statement of Work dated September 20, 2004, by the following paragraphs: 3.1.1 "Immersion," 3.1.2 "Scenario Generation," 3.1.3 "Content Creation," 3.1.4 "Graphics," 3.1.6 "Sound," 3.1.7 "Knowledge Integration," 3.1.8 "Creative Technologies," and 3.1.9 "Evaluation."

PART I – TECHNICAL PROPOSAL

1.0   TECHNICAL APPROACH

Background

Within the military population (which includes both warfighters and warfighter families), the need for health information is growing at an astounding rate. Recent statistics indicate that a growing percentage of military personnel are surviving wounds and injuries received in OIF/OEF compared to the conflicts of the past. For example, one report suggests that of all those wounded in Iraq, Afghanistan and nearby staging locations, there is a ratio of 16 wounded servicemen for every fatality. This compares with the Vietnam and Korean wars where there were 2.6 and 2.8 injuries per fatality, respectively, and WWs I and II, which had fewer than 2 wounded servicemen per death [1]. Advances in training, tactics, body/vehicle armor technology and military battlefield medicine have led to this unprecedented number of survivors of severe battlefield trauma. **However, along with these successes in force protection and survivability have come significant challenges in the form of providing health care for these brave survivors of trauma.** The challenges to be faced are daunting. In this regard, the recent report of a surge in military suicide rates has again thrust the challenges of military mental health care into the public spotlight. With annual suicide rates steadily rising since 2004, the month of January 2009 saw 24 suspected suicides, compared to five in January of 2008, six in January of 2007 and 10 in January of 2006 [2].

In spite of a Herculean effort on the part of the DOD to produce and disseminate behavioral health programs for military personnel and their families, the complexity of the issues involved continue to challenge the best efforts of military mental health care experts, administrators and providers. Since 2004, numerous blue ribbon panels of experts have attempted to assess the current DOD and VA healthcare delivery system and provide recommendations for improvement (DOD Mental Health Task Force [3], National Academies of Science Institute of Medicine [4], Dole-Shalala Commission Report [5], Rand Report [6], American Psychological Association [7]). Most of these reports cite a need for identification and implementation of ways to enhance the healthcare dissemination/delivery system for military personnel and their families in a fashion that provides better awareness and access to care while reducing the stigma of help-seeking.

For example, the American Psychological Association Presidential Task Force on Military Deployment Services for Youth, Families and Service Members [7] presented their preliminary report in February of 2007 which flatly stated that they were, "...not able to find any evidence of a well-coordinated or well-disseminated approach to providing behavioral health care to service members and their families." The APA report also went on to describe three primary barriers to military mental health treatment for both active duty members and families: availability, acceptability and accessibility. More specifically:

1. Well-trained mental health specialists are not in adequate supply (availability)
2. The military culture needs to be modified such that mental health services are more accepted and less stigmatized,

6

3. And even if providers were available and seeking treatment was deemed acceptable, appropriate mental health services are often not readily accessible due to a variety of factors (e.g. long waiting lists, limited clinic hours, a poor referral process and geographical location).

While advances in technology has begun to show promise for the creation of new and effective clinical assessment and treatment approaches -- from Virtual Reality to computerized prosthetics -- improvements in the military health care dissemination/delivery system are required to take full advantage of these evolving treatment methodologies, as well as for standard proven intervention options.

To address the above barriers, the University of Southern California (USC) Institute for Creative Technologies (ICT) proposes to develop and deliver an intelligent, interactive program referred to as SimCoach. The SimCoach experience will be designed to **attract** and **engage** Warfighters and Warfighter families who might not otherwise seek help (whether because of lack of awareness about or reluctance to utilize resources). **The goal will be to create an experience that will motivate these Warfighters and their families to take the first step – to empower themselves with regard to their healthcare** (e.g., psychological health and traumatic brain injury) **and general personal welfare** (i.e., other non-medical stressors such as economic or relationship issues) – and encourage them to take the next step towards other, more formal resources that are available. SimCoach will not be able to breakdown all the barriers identified above nor address the entire breadth of needs in the information space nor provide diagnostic or counseling services. SimCoach will aim to foster comfort and confidence in tackling the rest of the process.

Multi-Disciplinary Approach

As stated above, the goal of the SimCoach experience will be to attract and engage warfighters and warfighter families that might not otherwise seek help. A fundamental challenge of this project is to better understand this user base and their attitudes such that appropriate user experiences can be designed. This population is likely to be a diverse group of individuals with a myriad of needs. First, there are fundamental differences between the needs of warfighters and the warfighter families. This includes the functional challenges (e.g., the wounded warrior vs. the effects of the wounded warrior on the family when re-integrating; coping with the experience of war vs. not having any information to understand the experience of war; etc.). Second, within both populations, there are likely those who are not even aware that there are resources available that can help them (a subset of which may not even realize/understand their problem) and those who are aware but unwilling/unable to use the available resources. Third, attracting and engaging these individuals will likely require the availability/use of a variety of strategies and tactics. Among the things that the system will likely have to do is break down mistrust (e.g., openness, humor, peer reinforcement, etc), be helpful and productive for the user whether the user trusts the system, and keep the user coming back for continued assistance or until the user decides to seek assistance from a recommended care provider.

The intention of the SimCoach project is to leverage a variety of techniques to design the user experience. One source of knowledge is the medical/clinical practice. One potentially relevant clinical model is the PLISSIT clinical framework (**P**ermission, **L**imited **I**nformation, **S**pecific **S**uggestions, and **I**ntensive **T**herapy [8]), which provides an established model for encouraging help-seeking behaviors in persons who may feel stigma and insecurity regarding their condition. In the SimCoach project, we would likely only be able to address the "PLISS" components, leaving the intensive therapy component to live professionals that users could be referred to. Another potentially relevant model is the Trans-theoretical Model of Behavioral Change: (1) Pre-contemplation, (2) Contemplation, (3) Preparation, (4) Action, (5) Maintenance, (6) Termination. In this model, a person can be taken from stage 1 to stage 2 through consciousness raising, from stage 2 to stage 3 through self-reevaluation, and from stage 3 to stage 4 through lowering barriers.

Another source of knowledge is the social work practice. These models take a case management approach, serving as an advocate and guide. Social work input will be garnered via our collaboration with the USC School of Social Work and with internationally respected outside consultants. Finally, another source of knowledge is the entertainment/game practice. This community is not typically oriented towards healthcare. However, their models focus most explicitly on attracting and engaging individuals that can inform the design of a more friendly or otherwise appealing experience – to help get people "in the door." Entertainment and marketing techniques for engaging and/or influencing behavior include creating an experience that will result in the suspension of disbelief, "hooks" that motivate people to keep trying, and well-crafted messaging/experience that lead to a consistency that could lead to additional opportunities to retain the user.

ICT is uniquely positioned to provide expertise in each individual area and has demonstrated experience integrating these diverse considerations into a coherent, compelling, and ultimately effectively experience.

SimCoach Concept

SimCoach will be a part of a holistic experience designed to attract, engage, and empower the users. Users will ideally be able to access the system with a low-end computer and no special software (the desired platform is the web, but technical feasibility will need to be assessed to determine if the entire experience – especially the virtual humans – can be delivered through the web). The users will also be allowed to remain completely anonymous. When they arrive, the users will find a very simple launch point that will allow them to dig deeply into specific issues if they are already self-directed or to "wander around" to get comfortable with the system and/or the issues that they may (or may not) be facing. The user will likely be able to use the site without having to create a user account, but, if they wish to have some persistence, they will have the ability to create an account – though this account will also be totally anonymous if they so desire.

Initial design studies and focus group outputs will explore alternative approaches to designing the SimCoach user experience. To illustrate one form that the SimCoach experience could take, we have created a use example:

Maria was the 23-year old wife of Juan, an OIF veteran who had completed two deployments before leaving the service. After his return, she noticed something different. He had become distant, never discussed his experiences in Iraq, and when asked, he would answer, "that was then, this is now, case closed". He also wasn't as involved with their two children (the 2ⁿᵈ one was born while he was in Iraq), only playing with their oldest boy after hours of begging. For the most part, Juan stayed home and had yet begun to look for a civilian job. He didn't sleep much and when he did manage to fall asleep, he would often wake up after an hour, highly agitated claiming that he heard someone trying to get in the bedroom window. When this happened, he would sometimes sit till dawn, peering through slits in the closed blinds, watching for the "imaginary" intruder to return.

He seemed jumpy when not drinking and watching TV. He drank heavily during the day and Maria would often find him asleep or passed out on the couch when she got home from her job after picking the kids up from her mother's house. She told her mother that it felt like she was living with a ghost, but that she still loved him. She just wanted the "old Juan" back. However, each day things got worse and she was feeling like she couldn't live like this much more. She felt guilty for the increasing resentment that she felt but didn't know how (or was afraid) to talk to Juan about what she was feeling. Juan also kept a pistol in the house and one time she had moved it off the dresser while cleaning and when Juan couldn't find it, he went ballistic and ran frantically around the house, screaming, "how am I gonna protect my family without my weapon!"

Maria was at a loss as to what to do when her mother mentioned hearing on Oprah about a way to find help for these kinds of problems on the internet with a thing called "SimCoach". Maria had only occasionally "played" on the AOL games site before and she didn't own a computer, but her older sister's son was a "computer nut" and agreed to let her come over to use his computer and try out SimCoach. She couldn't understand how a computer could help her, but she was desperate for any help she could get. So her nephew showed her how to type in the address for www.simcoach.mil on his computer and then went out with his friends to a movie.

Maria was intrigued when the screen lit up and created the illusion of standing in front of a "craftsman"-like building with the sign above it reading, "DCOE Helpcenter". Immediately the "virtual" director of the center walked out onto the porch and beckoned her to come in. The director stated that "we are here to understand your needs and get you started on the path to help" and showed Maria a poster just inside the door that had images and short biographies of the staff. Pointing towards the poster, she said, "here is our staff, have a look and click on the picture of who you would feel comfortable meeting with." Maria paused when she noticed a staff member that reminded her of a teacher she had in high school who was always helpful and kind to her. She clicked on this picture and was then guided through the hallway of the center that actually looked quite warm and peaceful with virtual people in the hall smiling and talking to each other softly. The program whisked her into a room where Dr. Hartkis, sitting in a thick fabric chair next to a fireplace, smiled, and softly asked her how he could help. Maria knew that this was just a virtual human, but for some reason she felt comforted by his soft voice and kind facial expressions. She had never been to a clinician before for this kind of help and was surprised by how safe and comfortable she felt. Not knowing what to expect, she described how her husband, Juan, was having problems ever since he came back from the war. She was surprised when the doctor said in a reassuring voice, "If you want to tell me more about it, I think I can help you and your family." After requesting some basic information, Dr. Hartkis then asked Maria some questions that seemed like he really might "understand" some of what she was going through. Eventually, after answering a series of thoughtful questions, Dr. Hartkis reassuringly smiled and then pointed to a wall in the room and said, "Here are some websites that have information that is available to help folks that are going through what you are feeling. We can pull up one of them and take a look at what is available or I can find a care provider in or near your zip code that we can make an appointment with right now so you can begin to find the help that both you and Juan could benefit from. Or, if you're not ready for that yet, we can still talk more about what you're going through now."

Maria couldn't believe that this computer character seemed so genuine in his face and his manner, and that she felt like she wanted to tell him more. Perhaps he might really be able to get her started on the road to help both her and Juan? Suddenly she realized that she had been online for an hour and needed to go home. As she was leaving, she wondered aloud if she could think about the options that she learned about today and then come back to make a decision on what to do. Dr. Hartkis smiled and said, "Of course we can meet again…you see, I will always be here to guide you to the help you need, whenever you're ready."

In addition to such a direct, first person experience with a virtual human, the clinical team and focus groups will consider alternative user experiences. In particular, we will consider third person, case-based approaches used in systems like Carmen's Bright IDEAS [Marsella et al. 2000, 2003] that are designed to reduce the user's concerns about seeking help and discussing their problems. In such an approach, a virtual character like Dr. Hartkis would be discussing with a visitor, played by another virtual character, a problem that the visitor is having, providing information about possible avenues to address those problems. The user interacts with the system in order to tailor the exchange between Dr. Hartkis so it is similar to the difficulties the user is having.

SimCoach will support the creation of multiple virtual human characters and personalities. Some may not give advice at all. They may serve only to encourage or perhaps take more of a Socratic and/or Eliza approach, asking many questions that force the user to generate their own ideas. Others may be very fact- and information-based. For example, experts on specific clinical topics may convey healthcare information in an accurate and accessible fashion that does not come off as condescending. Some characters could be based on specific interests of the users – such as a virtual Tiger Woods that appeals to golfers who can find out more about how to use golf as a part of a medical or personal regimen. Other characters could be embodied as clinical military personnel, armed with first hand knowledge that is perceived by the user to be more relevant to their experience. Chaplain characters could also be created for those who would be more trusting of a coach that can present helpful content from a more spiritual background.. Input from the clinical team and output of early focus groups will serve to prioritize which classes of characters will be deployed for the initial implementation.

Based on information garnered through the interaction between the user and the virtual human, as well as the evocative design of the specific avatar, the user will be given appropriate levels of direct or indirect information or suggestions regarding access to relevant information on psychology, social work, neurology, rehabilitation, the military healthcare system, and also to other Service Members. Users will also be directed to experts on specific areas such as stress, brain injury, relationship counseling, substance abuse, suicide, rehabilitation, reintegration and other relevant specialties as appropriate.

In addition to interaction with avatars, the system will deliver complementary content that will augment the interactions with the characters. This could include edited content such as articles, video testimonials and blog posts as well as connection to peers and other support systems with real people through forums and community groups (on the site as in the model of CompanyCommand.com and/or available external groups on Facebook, garrison-focused resources such as the 10th MTN DIV community website, and non-profit support groups such as Military.com's forums).

There would also be options to allow the user to perform some simple neurocognitive and psychological tests to help inform self-awareness or aid in making decisions on initial referral options. Users will also have the option to print out a summary of the computerized sessions to bring with them when seeking medical treatment to enhance their comfort level, armed with knowledge, when dealing with human clinical care providers and experts.

Virtual Humans

A core piece of the SimCoach experience will be interactive Virtual Humans that users will be able to interact with. These virtual humans will be capable of speech, gestures and emotion. It is expected that there will be a variety of virtual humans (based on real people and fictional characters created specifically for this effort) available to serve the variety of needs of the target audience, so the virtual human architecture will be expected to support this variety. The virtual human will also be capable of "remembering" the user from the previous visits and build on that information in similar fashion to that of a growing human relationship.

The system will allow users to flexibly interact with this character by typing text, clicking on character generated menu options and, potentially, limited speech interaction during the initial phases of development. The specific interaction methods will have to be developed as a part of the design efforts based on a deep exploration of the user base and their needs. We will explore the feasibility of supporting as much natural language (typed and spoken) as possible – with short-term decisions made based on technical feasibility, risk mitigation, and the need to demonstrate capabilities even if they are not fully mature.

Several studies illustrate that such a use of VH technology can lead to greater user satisfaction and increased adherence to medical advice, however it is easy to get it wrong (c.f., Microsoft's "Clippy") and we will emphasize evaluation-driven design, with focus groups and laboratory studies driving the evolution towards final system design. The strongest evidence in support of our basic concept is a series of studies using virtual humans in health communication and medical adherence. In one study, patients were more likely to sign a medical consent form and were more satisfied with the consent process when a virtual human explained it compared with a human explainer [9]. In another study, hospital patients with low health-literacy preferred receiving discharge information from a virtual human over their own doctor or nurse [10]. However, several studies point to the need for caution and careful evaluation before fielding systems.   For example, a large body of research suggests that people may be less truthful disclosing medical information to a virtual human when compared with a simple web-based form [11]. Some evidence suggests that speech-based virtual human interaction is problematic for medical consultations given the current inability to recognizing nuanced speech [12] and text-based interaction may perform better. Other findings are mixed and point to the need to carefully control for character appearance and behavior. For example, several studies emphasize that character appearance, gender, race, weight and behavior can both positively and negatively impact perceived credibility and effectiveness of applications using virtual humans [13-16]. The proposal includes extensive evaluation efforts to mitigate the above risks, guide system design, and document the effectiveness of the final system.

Architecture

The software principle underlying the design of SimCoach is to create a backbone that can grow organically over time and does not tie the government to a single developer. We will design the software to be open, modular, and easy to extend and author content. Where possible, the system will incorporate open source modules and open standards to facilitate incorporation in a modular fashion to facilitate incorporation of the latest advances in language processing, graphics, artificial intelligence, and other technological requirements. A series of content development tools will facilitate the creation of new virtual human characters by non-technical clinicians so that the system can grow and expand over time with new experts and focus areas as required. We will create options for these VHs to be based on real people such that well-known experts and military figures could be integrated into the application if determined to be relevant by users and if image licenses do not drain inordinate resources from the project. We will explore capabilities to direct users to a monitored and moderated social networking site that would only be accessible by Service members and allow anonymous discussions of issues and problems being faced.

1.1   Primary Tasks/Subtasks

SimCoach is envisioned as a part of a system that will be safe, encouraging, and sympathetic. To create this experience, ICT will face a number of deep research and design challenges that will be addressed through a multi-disciplinary approach.

On the research side, some of these challenges involve incremental improvements to existing virtual human technology but several fundamental challenges are specific to this proposed application and overcoming them will likely result in fundamental contributions to the future design of computer-supported medical advice and treatment. The questions include:

- Virtual Humans: How can the appearance and behavior of virtual humans be implemented to produce the desired outcomes? How can virtual human technologies be adapted for the technical constraints of the SimCoach system?

12

- User Modeling: Can we develop techniques to infer the user's treatment needs but also their attitude towards treatment (e.g. are they avoidant? Are they denying the reality of their problem)? Can we detect changes in needs and attitudes through the course of their interaction with SimCoach? How do we best assess if users are adhering to prior advice?
- Authoring: What is the best way to elicit structured content from clinicians? How can non-technical experts author character dialogue and behaviors? What are the best ways to automatically or semi-automatically guide these elicitations?

On the design side, the challenges are particularly confounding since the target of SimCoach is a population that is not actively seeking resources.

- How do we structure the interaction to promote engagement?
- How do we craft character appearance and behaviors to instill rapport/therapeutic-alliance? What are the best/most appropriate roles for an embodied, intelligent virtual human character? How does the appearance and behavior of the character impact outcomes?
- How much or little information does the user have to provide before "engaging"?
- How do we adapt content based on our understanding of user needs and attitudes?
- How do we create outreach opportunities through features on the site? How do we incorporate complementary content such as blogs, community forums, and other community-building features to attract potential users?

As indicated by the above sets of questions, the research and design challenges are tightly related. The answers will be contingent on the capabilities afforded by the research and the needs of the design. ICT is uniquely positioned to address this challenge as a university-affiliated research center (UARC) with an acknowledged special capability in the development of immersive applications through its marrying of research (computer science, psychology, education) with content creation (Hollywood film, game design).

To address the above questions, ICT proposes the following tasks:

1. User-centered team: Conduct target audience research, vet DCoE target resources, provide input to content-creation process
    1.1. Establish teams
        - Establish User-centered team (Social workers, Psychologists, psychiatrists, occupational and physical therapists, medical professionals), brainstorm strategies, structure workflow assignments among consultants based on expertise
        - Establish SME team (Senior leaders (COs and 1SG, BN and BDE CDRs and CSMs), Junior leaders (especially NCOs, PLs), Family reps, Chaplains, finance officers) based on ICT contacts and recommendations from User-centered team

    1.2. Establish and execute focus group plan (PTSD, Depression, Family/Interpersonal issues)
        1.2.1. Investigate IRB requirements for expedited review of Focus Groups and Individual Interviews at USC, Camp Pendleton and Ft. Lewis
        1.2.2. Create general submission template for expedited review of Focus Groups/Individual interviews plan
        1.2.3. Define Focus Groups/Individual interviews of interest (Soldiers, Spouses, Other family members and friends)

13

1.2.4. Plan strategy for Focus Group/Individual interviews access and scheduling constraints
1.2.5. Design structure and process of Focus Groups/Individual interviews
1.2.6. Select and/or develop structured assessment devices (Open-ended interview questions, paper and pencil questionnaires, online surveys, virtual human character stimuli)
1.2.7. Compile and final review all Focus Group/Individual interview content to be used
1.2.8. Submit all needed IRB expedited review proposals at all sites
1.2.9. Expedited IRB approval certified
1.2.10.Commence Focus Groups/Individual interviews at Camp Pendleton and Ft. Lewis
1.2.11.Compile Focus Groups/Individual interview data available at that point in time and put into report for distribution to all members of team

1.3. Establish and execute focus group plan (TBI/Addictions domain)
1.3.1. Review Focus Group/Individual interviews for elements relevant to TBI/Addictions domain
1.3.2. Compile Focus Groups/Individual interview data on TBI/Addictions and put into report for distribution to all members of team
1.3.3. Design Formative and Summative evaluation methodology for TBI/Addictions Prototype informed by methodology created for PTSD, Depression, Family and Interpersonal Issues experience.
1.3.4. Conduct Formative and Summative evaluation for TBI/Addictions module in YEAR 3

1.4. Investigate and enhance existing DCoE affiliated web-based content
1.4.1. Finalize DCoE web-based sites of interest for investigation and evaluation
1.4.2. Create method with consultants for investigating and evaluating existing DCoE affiliated web-based content for suitability for SimCoach referral.
1.4.3. Assign predetermined DCoE affiliated and other website content to consultants based on interest and area of expertise for investigation and evaluation
1.4.4. Extract data elements of relevance from Focus Groups/Individual interviews continuously in parallel with acquisition and creation of database of content for analysis.
1.4.5. Review progress on DCoE website content analysis from consultants
1.4.6. Integrate Findings from DCoE website analysis with Focus Groups/Individual interview data to create a structure for vetted content matched to needs and interests expressed by targeted users.
1.4.7. Assign predetermined DCoE affiliated and other website content to consultants based on interest and area of expertise for investigation and evaluation for TBI/Addictions domain
1.4.8. Analysis and organization of DCoE TBI/Addictions content by consultants
1.4.9. Review progress on DCoE TBI/Addictions website content analysis from consultants
1.4.10.Integrate Findings from DCoE TBI/Addictions website analysis with Focus Groups/Individual interview data to create a structure for vetted content matched to needs and interests expressed by targeted users.

1.5. Dialog development with user-centered consultants to feed production team
1.5.1. Commence informal dialog development with user-centered consultants for areas agreed to be mission critical areas for SimCoach functionality

1.5.2. Commence formalized development of dialog options
1.5.3. Incrementally deliver dialog content to production team
    1.5.3.1. Deliver basic demographic and history dialog
    1.5.3.2. Deliver PTSD dialog
    1.5.3.3. Deliver Depression dialog
    1.5.3.4. Deliver Family and Interpersonal issues dialog
1.5.4. Commence development of TBI and Addiction Module content
1.5.5. Commence informal TBI/Addictions dialog development with user-centered consultants for areas agreed to be mission critical areas for SimCoach functionality

14

1.5.6. Commence formalized development of TBI/Addictions dialog options

1.5.7. Incrementally deliver dialog content to production team

    1.5.7.1. Deliver TBI dialog

    1.5.7.2. Deliver Addictions dialog

1.6. Provide user-centered team feedback

    1.6.1. Examine and review Simcoach Version 1 prototype

- Provide Suggestions for changes in SimCoach content

    1.6.2. Examine and review SimCoach TBI/Addictions prototype

- Suggestions for changes in SimCoach TBI/Addictions content

2. Research and Design user experience

Effectively eliciting user information needs and disseminating health-care information requires an understanding of both the clinical problem and the current limitations of virtual human technology. This includes both interactions with virtual characters but, more broadly, with content and services that reside outside interactions with particular characters.

    2.1. Design overall user experience

- Specify how user interaction with SimCoach is initiated/maintained/terminated
- Identify the relationship between the portal, the virtual personas, and other SimCoach services
- Develop overarching themes and messages/"brand" of the site
- Foster/build complementary community

    2.2. Design user interaction with virtual personas

- Specify form of user/persona interaction: e.g., user-initiated/ system-initiated/mixed-initiative
- Specify modality of interaction: menu-based/text based
- Design strategies for eliciting user's demographic and clinical information

    2.3. Research, development and assessment of advanced interaction management

- User modeling to inform interaction
- Modeling of persistent relation between user and virtual to inform interaction
- Persuasive tactics to induce learner to seek help
- Empirical studies on impact of interaction techniques on user self-disclosure and advice adherence

    2.4. Develop promo video and other complementary materials for communicating need and vision to decision-makers, people who can provide input, and other stakeholders

3. Content creation

    3.1. Design information architecture (oriented towards service-oriented architecture model)

The target clinical domain comprises a wealth of knowledge and it will be necessary to formally describe a subset of this in a functional taxonomy. The architecture will relate community/clinical knowledge to representational structures ultimately consumed by software tools and virtual human agents. Where possible, semantic web standards will be used to maximize future interoperability.

      3.1.1. Design open information architecture and tools that will facilitate development of content by other developers.

        3.1.1.1. Collect and compile candidate online resources for mental health and TBI content starting with DCoE affiliated sites (including *Battlemind* and *After-Deployment*).

        3.1.1.2. Review and vet content from candidate sites by SMEs.

3.1.2.   Specify needed classes of information sources including internal content (e.g., information on clinical conditions and social support) and external content (e.g., relevant military and civilian web portal)

3.1.3.   Develop information ontology and indexes to structure content creation and retrieval

3.1.4.   Develop architecture/ontology for virtual human interactions (e.g., advice giving, rapport-building, empathetic, Socratic, etc) – that informs development of specific virtual human agents and authoring by others (service API)

3.1.5.   Develop an integrative content workflow model that informs development of the content pipeline and authoring tools (service API)

Content development will span geographically-separated teams as well as disciplines (Tasks 1.4, 1.5, 3.2) necessitating a robust workflow process with checks and balances. Tools that support these distributed teams will be developed in 4.2.3.

3.1.6.   Identify/provide user-editable content (blogs)

3.1.7.   Foster/moderate community content (forums/support groups)

3.2. Content production

An ongoing task to develop the virtual human avatar models and art dependencies; virtual human dialogue content and behavior models (e.g. advice-giving tactics, interaction goals); and static clinical content to populate the online repository.

    3.2.1. Virtual human art asset production

        3.2.1.1. Concept design artwork

        3.2.1.2. Modeling

        3.2.1.3. Rigging

        3.2.1.4. Texturing

        3.2.1.5. Animation

        3.2.1.6. Voice recording and syncing

    3.2.2. Authoring of dialogue and behavior models

Dialogue authoring begins with the writing of representative transcripts and wizard of oz studies from task 1.5. Information taxonomies and processes developed in 3.3 and the content generation tools developed in 4.2.3 form the basis for actual content authoring by both the user-centered and production team. Content is deployed to the virtual human runtime architecture for initial testing and analysis by the production team.

        3.2.2.1. Authoring of auxiliary clinical content: e.g., limited information, specific suggestions

4. Development

4.1. Develop system architecture (oriented towards service-oriented architecture model)

The runtime system will be developed using a service-oriented architecture approach utilizing recognized enterprise design patterns (e.g. service model, loose-coupling) and interoperability standards (e.g. http, xml, messaging transports). The service approach will promote future re-use and interoperability with external systems that are separately developed. A critical task for this effort is the successful "service-ization" of existing virtual human component technologies suitable for an enterprise (e.g. web) environment. Additionally, a set of application-level services representing and managing the user interaction logic, user preferences, and presentation will be developed. The SimCoach web application will harvest and utilize these newly developed services.

    4.1.1. Identify available, required, and/or ready technologies to service the design

        4.1.1.1. Core services (Interaction manager, animation)

        4.1.1.2. Support services (Messaging, web content delivery, web application container, identity manager, database)

The SimCoach web application will utilize a standards-based industry enterprise platform (e.g. J2EE, Microsoft .NET) for realizing, deploying and hosting component services. The specific vendor selection may change throughout the project but every attempt will be made to remain platform-neutral by utilizing standards.

4.1.1.3. Virtual human component services (Dialogue manager, non-verbal behavior, reasoning and decision-making)
    4.1.2. Develop service definitions
A service definition is the specification of the application "contract" between the service-provider and service-client (e.g. similar to an application programming interface or API). Defining the information exchange requirements early in the project allows for independent team development of individual component services designed to interoperate with well-defined services.
  4.2. Develop components
    4.2.1. Develop web application
The SimCoach web application will comprise the overall experience designed in 2.1. The web application is hosted on the support services layer and provides the implementation of the user interface and the application logic driving the interaction with the virtual human (e.g. session initialization and configuration, turn-by-turn interaction, logging, and session resume/end management).
      4.2.1.1. Presentation / UI
      4.2.1.2. Interaction manager application logic
      4.2.1.3. Virtual human integration APIs
      4.2.1.4. Persistent data models and external resource frameworks (personalization)
    4.2.2. Develop/port virtual human components
Existing virtual human technical components require development effort to "wrap" them as services. Most existing components are deployed for rich, non-web IT environments and certain optimizations will be necessary to support deployment as enterprise services.
      4.2.2.1. Smartbody service wrapping
      4.2.2.2. Smartbody web client
      4.2.2.3. Dialogue manager
      4.2.2.4. ASR/ NLU service wrapping
    4.2.3. Develop content pipeline and authoring tools
Content development tools and associated processes will be developed early in the project first to support internal development but later to serve as the basis for end-user authoring tools. This content framework will likely utilize a service model and will utilize a web-based interface where practical. Certain tools (e.g. avatar creation, audio recording) may be developed as standalone applications.
    4.2.4. Develop web-based administration tools
    4.2.5. Virtual human subsystem development and advanced capabilities
      4.2.5.1. Improve nonverbal behavior controllers
        4.2.5.1.1. Improved face and gesture controllers
        4.2.5.1.2. Application-specific enhancements to nonverbal generation rules
      4.2.5.2. Offline version of SmartBody animation system suitable for Web delivery
      4.2.5.3. Expressive speech synthesis (CMU)
        4.2.5.3.1. Initial general CMU Flite-platform voice
        4.2.5.3.2. Delivery of 2 additional voices
        4.2.5.3.3. Research and development of emotional/stylistic techniques
      4.2.5.4. Improved dialogue-management and language understanding
A web application for the administration of user accounts and access control will be developed to support ongoing maintenance of the deployed web application.
  4.3. System integration and testing

5.   Assessment: The effectiveness of SimCoach will be informed and assessed by a series of formative and summative evaluations. Formative evaluations will assess the viability and impact of system design choices through focus groups and individual tests, with relevant target users similar in nature to the users involved in the initial focus group/individual interviews conducted from Month 4 onward, and more formal laboratory studies. Summative evaluations will assess user experience with the overall system.
  5.1. Design strategy and methodology for formative evaluation of SimCoach Prototype 1 (PTSD/Depression/Family and Interpersonal issues)

5.1.1. Select and/or develop structured assessment devices (Open-ended interview questions, paper and pencil questionnaires, online surveys, and behavioral tests

5.2. Focus group and individual interviews

5.2.1. User groups rating possible character personas

5.2.1.1. Physical appearance

5.2.1.2. Social role (clinician, soldier, family member)

5.2.1.3. Character voice and diction

5.2.2. Interaction modality (e.g., menu vs. text vs. voice)

5.2.3. Qualitative assessment of reported life challenges

5.3. Conduct Formative user testing with Prototype 1 system for design/development support

5.3.1. Assess ability of system to establish rapport, promote self-disclosure

5.3.2. Assess impact of advanced emotionally-expressive avatars

5.3.3. Assess preference, likeability, likelihood for return use

5.3.4. Collect qualitative user feedback for possible inclusion in revised version

5.3.5. Quality Assurance

5.4. Compile and analyze data from Formative evaluation results and report on results for improving next prototype (Months 17-18).

5.5. Design Summative evaluation methodology for SimCoach Prototype 1 (PTSD, Depression, Family and Interpersonal issues modules)

5.6. Conduct effectiveness assessment (or Summative Evaluation) of PTSD, Depression and Family and Interpersonal Issues Module

5.6.1. Engagement of users

5.6.2. Behavior change of users

5.6.3. Attitudes of users

5.6.4. Clinical effects

5.6.5. Impact of embodied interface on user self-disclosure and satisfaction

5.6.6. Impact of spoken vs. typed speech on user satisfaction and quality of elicited information

5.7. Conduct Formative and Summative evaluation of TBI/Addictions Module in YEAR 3

1.2   Relation to Other ICT Projects

Virtual Humans – We will build SimCoach by using existing ICT virtual human technology.

ICT's respected experience and success in developing compelling experiences that provide structured experiences will be key to the development of SimCoach. ICT will leverage its organizational knowledge and, as appropriate, technical elements developed under the BiLAT project. BiLAT is a large-scale (10 characters, 15 meetings) scenario wherein students practice conducting bi-lateral negotiations in a cultural context. The system was developed for the Unreal Engine and runs on a single computer. BiLAT has been used in pre-deployment training with the 10th MTN DIV, 101st ABN DIV, and 1ID, and is being deployed across the Army by TCM Gaming and PEO STRI.

ICT's ability to develop realistic and relevant content will be another critical element for the development of SimCoach. ICT will leverage its experience and knowledge gained from the Army Excellence Leadership (AXL) project. AXL is aimed at accelerating the acquisition of tacit knowledge of interpersonal military leadership issues through the development of compelling filmed case studies and interactive technologies. This effort is a collaboration with the U.S. Army Research Institute for Behavioral and Social Sciences (ARI) Fort Leavenworth

Research Unit (FLRU). Particularly relevant is the work developing AXL filmed scenarios focused on battlefield ethics. Funded by the U.S. Army Corps of Chaplains, ICT developed two scenarios, one targeted at lower enlisted (E2-E4) and one targeted at NCOs and junior officers. The films provide compelling, realistic scenarios that provoke discussion within units about the "grey areas" of challenging, ethically-relevant decisions. The films have been shown to a wide range of MOSs, ranks, and deployment experiences, and overall all have found the films to be very realistic and relevant. The films are in the process of being distributed across the Army.

ICT will also leverage the significant mental health and rehabilitation expertise that is available at the center and from other USC departments. The ICT VRPSYCH Lab has considerable experience in the design, development and evaluation of Clinical Virtual Reality applications dating back to 1996. The research and development from this group has lead to the creation of advanced simulation tools for PTSD Exposure Therapy (Virtual Iraq), Neuropsychological Assessment (VRCPAT), Physical/Occuapational Therapy Rehabilitation (NIDRR-RERC) and the lab has pioneered in the application of Virtual human patients for training novice clinicians on how to conduct sensitive diagnostic interviews with patients having challenging clinical disorders. This expertise is supplemented by long-standing collaborative relationships with USC colleagues in social work, psychology, occupational therapy, physical therapy, in addition to a well formed network of colleagues from other institutions who will serve as consultants on the project.

We will draw on ICT core competences in computer science, artificial intelligence, natural language processing, graphics, software engineering, human computer interaction, clinical psychology, neuropsychology, physical therapy and intelligent tutoring.

1.3   Army and/or DoD Relevance

The need for military-specific health information is growing at an astounding rate. Recent statistics indicate that a growing percentage of military personnel are surviving wounds and injuries received in OIF/OEF compared to the conflicts of the past. For example, one report suggests that of all those wounded in Iraq, Afghanistan and nearby staging locations – there is a ratio of 16 wounded servicemen for every fatality. This compares with the Vietnam and Korean wars where there were 2.6 and 2.8 injuries per fatality, respectively, and WWs I and II, which had fewer than 2 wounded servicemen per death [1]. Advances in training, tactics, body/vehicle armor technology and military battlefield medicine have led to this unprecedented number of survivors of severe battlefield trauma. However, along with these successes in force protection and survivability have come significant challenges in the form of providing health care for these brave survivors of trauma. In this regard, the recent report of a surge in Army suicide rates has again thrust the challenges of military mental health care into the public spotlight. With annual suicide rates steadily rising since 2004, the month of January, 2009 saw 24 suspected suicides, compared to five in January of 2008, six in January of 2007 and 10 in January of 2006 [2]. In spite of a Herculean effort on the part of the DOD to produce and disseminate behavioral health programs for military personnel and their families, the complexity of the issues involved continue to challenge the best efforts of military mental health care experts, administrators and providers. Since 2004, numerous blue ribbon panels of experts have attempted to assess the current DOD and VA healthcare delivery system and provide recommendations for improvement

(DOD Mental Health Task Force [3], National Academies of Science Institute of Medicine [4], Dole-Shalala Commission Report [5], Rand Report [6], American Psychological Association [7]). Most of these reports cite two major areas in need of improvement:

1. Support for randomized controlled trials that test the efficacy of treatment methodologies, leading to wider dissemination of evidenced based approaches
2. Identification and implementation of ways to enhance the healthcare dissemination/delivery system for military personnel and their families in a fashion that provides better awareness and access to care while reducing the stigma of help-seeking.

For example, the *American Psychological Association Presidential Task Force on Military Deployment Services for Youth, Families and Service Members* [7] presented their preliminary report in February of 2007 which flatly stated that they were, "*...not able to find any evidence of a well-coordinated or well-disseminated approach to providing behavioral health care to service members and their families.*" The APA report also went on to describe three primary barriers to military mental health treatment for both active duty members and families: *availability, acceptability and accessibility.* More specifically:

1. Well-trained mental health specialists are not in adequate supply (*availability*)
2. The military culture needs to be modified such that mental health services are more *accepted* and less stigmatized,
3. And even if providers were available and seeking treatment was deemed acceptable, appropriate mental health services are often not readily *accessible* due to a variety of factors (e.g. long waiting lists, limited clinic hours, a poor referral process and geographical location).

Advanced technology has begun to show promise for the creation of new and effective clinical assessment and treatment approaches, from virtual reality to computerized prosthetics. It is now time for the military health care dissemination/delivery system to benefit from similar advances in communication and information technology to reduce stigma, enhance awareness of healthcare services and promote access. While extant traditional Internet and website options have greatly improved the potential *availability* of health-related media content, the SimCoach system with take this information the extra mile by enhancing *access* to these services by directly acknowledging barriers to care and addressing the needs of this very special user group by the breaking down of those barriers.

1.4   Related Work

With the continuing challenges that have emerged in military mental health and rehabilitative care, the DOD has set up the Defense Centers of Excellence for Psychological Health and Traumatic Brain Injury (DCoE) to provide a central organization for promoting better research and services (http://dcoe.health.mil/default.aspx). The DCoE establishes quality standards for: clinical care; education and training; prevention; patient, family and community outreach; and program excellence. Its mission is to maximize opportunities for military personnel and families to thrive through a collaborative global network promoting resilience, recovery, and reintegration for psychological health and traumatic brain injury. The following contains descriptions of each of the six primary affiliated DCoE sites as presented online.

Defense and Veterans Brain Injury Center (DVBIC) (http://www.dvbic.org/)
Funded through the U.S. Department of Defense, the mission of the Defense and Veterans Brain Injury Center (DVBIC) is to serve active duty military, their dependents and veterans with traumatic brain injury (TBI) through state-of-the-art medical care, innovative clinical research initiatives and educational programs. Originally established in 1992 as the "Defense and Veterans Head Injury Program," DVBIC is a multi-site medical care, clinical research and education center that consists of a unique collaboration of the Department of Defense (DoD), Department of Veterans Affairs (VA) health care system, and civilian partners. The site is well organized and provides an excellent collection of resources and links.

Center for Deployment Psychology (http://www.deploymentpsych.org/)
The Center for Deployment Psychology was developed to promote the education of psychologists and other behavioral health specialists about issues pertaining to the deployment of military personnel. The CDP is a tri-service center funded by Congress to train military and civilian psychologists, psychology interns/residents, and other behavioral health professionals to provide high quality deployment-related behavioral healthservices to military personnel and their families. The site provides useful links to information sheets, books and articles, course resources and information about upcoming training events.

Deployment Health Clinical Center (http://www.pdhealth.mil/)
This site was designed "to assist clinicians in the delivery of post-deployment healthcare by fostering a trusting partnership between military men and women, veterans, their families, and their healthcare providers to ensure the highest quality care for those who make sacrifices in the world's most hazardous workplace." This site has a many resources hidden in links with titles that may not be so familiar to civilian clinicians. For example, the RESPECT-Mil link has an excellent collection of downloadable manuals and in the Library link there is also access to many useful forms and assessment devices.

Center   for   the   Study   of   Traumatic   Stress
(http://www.centerforthestudyoftraumaticstress.org/home.shtml)
The Center for the Study of Traumatic Stress conducts research, education, consultation and training on preparing for and responding to the psychological effects and health consequences of traumatic events. These events include natural (hurricanes, floods and tsunami) and human made disasters (motor vehicle and plane crashes, war, terrorism and bioterrorism). The Center's work spans studies of genetic vulnerability to stress, individual and community responses to terrorism, and policy recommendations to help our nation and its military and civilian populations. The Center is part of the Uniformed Services University of the Health Sciences, Department of Psychiatry and was established in 1987 as a public private partnership of USUHS and the Henry M. Jackson Foundation for the Advancement of Military Medicine. The Center's approach integrates science, clinical care, community needs and the health of the nation. Its team is multi-disciplinary with expertise in disaster psychiatry, military medicine and psychiatry, social and organizational psychology, neuroscience, family violence, workplace preparedness and public education. This work has now generated an unprecedented body of research, scholarship and one

of the world's largest databases (over 18,000 articles) on psychological, social and behavioral consequences of exposure to traumatic events and other extreme environments (e.g., desert, space, undersea). This includes mental health responses ranging from resilience, distress, health risk behaviors, disaster behaviors and psychiatric illness such as post-traumatic stress disorder, acute stress disorder and depression. Needless to say, this site is filled with many useful downloadable items.

National Center for Telehealth & Technology (*http://www.t2health.org/*)
The National Center for Telehealth and Technology (T2) researches, develops, evaluates, and deploys new and existing technologies for Psychological Health (PH) and Traumatic Brain Injury (TBI) across the Department of Defense (DoD). The T2 Center meets this mission by serving as the principal DoD coordinator in such areas as innovative technology applications, suicide surveillance and prevention, online behavioral health tools, and telepsychological health. The site provides a great overview of the various DOD program efforts that apply VR and associated technologies to address military healthcare needs.

After Deployment (http://afterdeployment.org/)
After Deployment aims to assist military personnel and their loved ones with managing the challenges that are often faced following a deployment. The site provides information and self-guided solutions for dealing with post-traumatic stress and war memories; conflict at work; depression; anger; sleep problems; alcohol and drug abuse; stress; relationship problems; kids and deployment; spiritual guidance and fitness; living with physical injuries; and health and wellness.

Battlemind (https://www.battlemind.army.mil/)
Quoting directly from the site: "Battlemind Training is the US Army's integrated mental health training program. The Battlemind Training system encompasses training targeted for all phases of the deployment cycle as well as the Warrior life cycle and medical education system. There is training designed for Warriors, Leaders, and military spouses. Battlemind Training reflects a strength-based approach, utilizing buddy aid and focusing on the leader's role in maintaining Warriors mental health. The word "Battlemind" was coined by GEN Crosby Saint, Commander-in-Chief, US Army, Europe in 1992 when he released a message entitled "Battlemind Guidelines for Battalion Commanders." GEN Saint's message described Battlemind as "a warrior's fortitude in the face of danger". Thus, Battlemind was originally a concept created by the warfighter for the warfighter. In 1998, as commander of the US Army Medical Research Unit-Europe, an overseas laboratory of the Walter Reed Army Institute of Research (WRAIR), then-MAJ Carl Castro read about Battlemind and recognized the relevancy for the Army at large. Soon after, LTC Castro and COL Charles Hoge, Director, Division of Psychiatry and Neurosciences, WRAIR, began discussing what mental health training should look like for Warriors returning from Iraq and Afghanistan. These discussions served as the impetus of what is now known as Battlemind Training. In fact, the first conceptualization of this mental health training was created by LTC Castro and COL Hoge while on a plane ride back to Washington D.C. following their briefing to senior leaders at the Army War College in Fort Leavenworth. Post-deployment Battlemind Training, including the creation of the Battlemind acronym, the topic areas and the actions, was then developed by COL Castro, COL Hoge, Dr.

Amy Adler, US Army Medical Research Unit-Europe, WRAIR, and Dr. Steven Messer, Department of Military Psychiatry, WRAIR."

The National Center for PTSD (http://www.ncptsd.va.gov/ncmain/index.jsp)
The National Center for PTSD is a center of excellence for research & education on the prevention, understanding, and treatment of PTSD. There are seven divisions across the country. Although the center does not provide direct clinical care, the center's mission is to advance the clinical care and social welfare of America's veterans through research, education, and training in the science, diagnosis, and treatment of PTSD and stress-related disorders. Its vision is to be the foremost leader in information on PTSD and trauma; information generated internally through its extensive research program, and information synthesized from published scientific research and collective clinical experience that is efficiently disseminated to the field. The Center is organized to facilitate rapid translation of science into practice, assuring that the latest research findings inform clinical care; and translation of practice into science, assuring that questions raised by clinical challenges are addressed using rigorous experimental protocols. By drawing on the specific expertise vested at each separate division (e.g., behavioral, neuroscientific, etc.), the National Center provides a unique infrastructure within which to implement multidisciplinary initiatives regarding the etiology, pathophysiology, diagnosis and treatment of PTSD. The NCPTSD site is literally filled with content in support of this mission and there is extensive downloadable content.

1.5   Plan for Collaboration and Leveraging Related Work

As identified above, the project will require collaboration with a multi-disciplinary group of individuals. ICT expects to draw on its own experts in those areas as well as those available through its relationship with the university, specifically the School of Social Work.

Externally, ICT expects to leverage DCoE's six affiliated center sites related to these issues -- Defense and Veterans Brain Injury Center, Center for Deployment Psychology, Deployment Health Clinical Center, Center for the Study of Traumatic Stress, National Intrepid Center of Excellence, and National Center for Telehealth & Technology, as well as such sites as *After Deployment*, *Battlemind* and the *National Center for PTSD*.

1.6   Deliverables

As described in SOW.

2.0   SPECIAL TECHNICAL FACTORS

2.1   Capabilities and Relevant Experience

2.1.1   Research Staff

Albert "Skip" Rizzo received his Ph.D. in Clinical Psychology from the State University of New York at Binghamton. He is a Research Scientist at the University of Southern California Institute for Creative Technologies and has Research Professor appointments with the USC Dept. of Psychiatry and Behavioral Sciences, and at the School of Gerontology. Dr. Rizzo conducts research on the design, development and evaluation of Virtual Reality systems targeting the areas of clinical assessment, treatment and rehabilitation. This work spans the domains of psychological, cognitive and motor functioning in both healthy and clinical populations. In the psychological domain, a recent project has focused on the translation of the graphic assets from the Xbox game, Full Spectrum Warrior, into an exposure therapy application for combat-related PTSD with Iraq War veterans. Additionally, he is conducting research on VR applications that use 360 Degree Panoramic video for exposure therapy (social phobia), role-playing applications (anger management, etc.). He is also working with a team that is creating artificially intelligent virtual patients that clinicians can use to practice skills required for challenging clinical interviews and diagnostic assessments (sexual assault, resistant patients, suicide lethality, etc.). His cognitive work has addressed the use of VR applications to test and train attention, memory, visuospatial abilities and executive function. In the motor domain, he has developed VR game systems to address physical rehabilitation post- stroke, spinal cord injury and traumatic brain injury, prosthetic use training and for general repair of impairments due chronic improper ergonomic activity in persons aging with and into disability within the NIDRR-funded USC Rehabilitation Engineering Research Center. He is also investigating the use of VR for pain distraction at LA Children's Hospital and is currently designing game-based VR scenarios to address issues of concern with children having autistic spectrum disorder. His research also involves designing and evaluating 3D User Interface devices and interaction methods and he has created a graduate level Industrial and Systems Engineering course at USC entitled, "Human Factors and Integrated Media Systems". In the area of Gerontology, Dr. Rizzo has served as the program director of the USC Alzheimer's Disease Research Center and is the creator of the Memory Enhancement Seminars for Seniors (MESS) program at the USC School of Gerontology. The MESS program is an 8-week series of seminars designed to assist older persons in learning the skills for memory maintenance and enhancement.

Stacy C. Marsella is a project leader at USC's Institute for Creative Technologies (ICT), a Research Associate Professor in the Department of Computer Science and a co-director of USC's Computational Emotion Group. He has a Ph.D. in Computer Science from Rutgers University and is well known for his work in computational models of human cognition, emotion and social behavior. He also works on incorporating these models into virtual humans, autonomous characters that look human, act like humans and can interact with humans within virtual worlds. He also has extensive experience in the design and construction of simulations of social interaction for a variety of research, training and military analysis applications. This includes his work on virtual humans used in immersive training environments. He is co-developer of EMA and the developer of PsychSim, a model of social influence based on theory-

24

of-mind modeling. He has also worked on psychotherapeutic applications of emotion models, including his work on Carmen's Bright Ideas, a system that teaches coping strategies to parents of cancer patients. He plays a leadership role in organizing workshops on virtual humans, social intelligence and emotion modeling. He is on the editorial board of the Journal of Experimental & Theoretical Artificial Intelligence, a member of the International Society for Research on Emotions (ISRE) and has published over 100 technical articles.

Dr. Jonathan Gratch (http://www.ict.usc.edu/~gratch) is an Associate Director for Virtual Humans Research at the University of Southern California's (USC) Institute for Creative Technologies, Research Associate Professor in the Department of Computer Science and co-director of USC's Computational Emotion Group. He completed his Ph.D. in Computer Science at the University of Illinois in Urban-Champaign in 1995. Dr. Gratch's research focuses on virtual humans (artificially intelligent agents embodied in a human-like graphical body), and computational models of emotion. He studies the relationship between cognition and emotion, the cognitive processes underlying emotional responses, and the influence of emotion on decision making and physical behavior. A recent emphasis of this work is on social emotions, emphasizing the role of contingent nonverbal behavior in the co-construction of emotional trajectories between interaction partners. His research has been supported by the National Science Foundation, DARPA, AFOSR and RDECOM. He is on the editorial board of the journal *Emotion Review* and is the President-Elect of the HUMAINE association, the international association on emotion and human-computer interaction. He is sitting member of the organizing committee for the International Conference on Intelligent Virtual Agents (IVA) and frequent organizer of conferences and workshops on emotion and virtual humans. He belongs to the American Association for Artificial Intelligence (AAAI) and the International Society for Research on Emotion. Dr. Gratch is the author of over 100 technical articles.

Julia M. Kim is a Project Director at the University of Southern California's Institute for Creative Technologies (ICT). Ms. Kim oversees multi-disciplinary efforts that integrate technology and media in innovative and useful ways for training and education. Ms. Kim oversees the Army Excellence in Leadership (AXL) project, a collaboration with the U.S. Army Research Institute's Ft. Leavenworth Research Unit (Leader Development). AXL combines original film-based cases with a a web-based case method teaching system for distributed/blended environments. Ms. Kim oversees the on-going development of ELECT BiLAT, a suite of immersive technology tools for training negotiation and leader meetings in a cross-cultural environment. The effort is a collaboration with Army agencies, educational psychologists, and game design experts. She is or has been the project leader for the ArmyFIT, Case Method Authoring Tools (CMAT), Socio-Cultural Interactive Training (SCIL) System, and Emergency Management Interactive Trainer (EMIT) projects.

2.1.2 *Facilities and Resources*

Institute for Creative Technologies

The Institute for Creative Technologies (ICT), as an interdisciplinary laboratory devoted to the advancement of virtual reality training applications, provides a unique and supportive environment for the advancement of virtual human technology. No other laboratory in the world has such ready access to world class talent across the range of disciplines that impact virtual human design: computer graphics, computer animation, computer games, audio rendering, artificial intelligence, natural language processing, and Hollywood/game industry professional content producers (graphic artists, CGI animators, audio engineers, writers, actors, etc.). The ICT includes state-of-the-art VR installations, including the Virtual Reality Theatre and FlatWorld. The VR Theatre uses high-resolution graphics and spatialized sound to immerse the participants in a simulated setting. An SGI Onyx Reality Monster IR3 (16 processors and 4 graphics pipes) generates the images, which three Barco 909 projectors project onto a curved screen that is 8.75 feet high and 31.3 feet wide. FlatWorld is a mixed reality simulation environment, merging cinematic stagecraft techniques with immersive media technology. There is equipment for high-resolution digital photography, digital video, and calibration. In addition, there are specialized project systems for distributed rendering, environment capture, and reflectance field measurement. A new device we have is our Light Stage, a 10-foot-diameter spherical device designed to illuminate and photograph an object or person's face from a dense set of lighting directions and viewing angles; it can also capture object geometry through structured lighting. In addition, the Institute contains laboratories for software development and user studies, including networked Windows, Macintosh and UNIX workstations (Sun, Solaris, SGI, and Linux). Software includes a variety of virtual human, simulation, and natural language dialogue systems.

2.2   Previous or Current Relevant Research and Development (R&D) Work

Virtual Humans

ICT's respected experience and success in developing compelling experiences that provide structured experiences will be key to the development of SimCoach. ICT will leverage its organizational knowledge and, as appropriate, technical elements developed under the BiLAT project. BiLAT is a large-scale (10 characters, 15 meetings) scenario wherein students practice conducting bi-lateral negotiations in a cultural context. The system was developed for the Unreal Engine and runs on a single computer. BiLAT has been used in pre-deployment training with the 10th MTN DIV, 101st ABN DIV, and 1ID, and is being deployed across the Army by TCM Gaming and PEO STRI.

ICT's ability to develop realistic and relevant content will be another critical element for the development of SimCoach. ICT will leverage its experience and knowledge gained from the Army Excellence Leadership (AXL) project. AXL is aimed at accelerating the acquisition of tacit knowledge of interpersonal military leadership issues through the development of

26

compelling filmed case studies and interactive technologies. This effort is a collaboration with the U.S. Army Research Institute for Behavioral and Social Sciences (ARI) Fort Leavenworth Research Unit (FLRU). Particularly relevant is the work developing AXL filmed scenarios focused on battlefield ethics. Funded by the U.S. Army Corps of Chaplains, ICT developed two scenarios, one targeted at lower enlisted (E2-E4) and one targeted at NCOs and junior officers. The films provide compelling, realistic scenarios that provoke discussion within units about the "grey areas" of challenging, ethically-relevant decisions. The films have been shown to a wide range of MOSs, ranks, and deployment experiences, and overall all have found the films to be very realistic and relevant. The films are in the process of being distributed across the Army.

2.3   Related Government Contracts

The SimCoach project technical development is most related to a variety of ICT Virtual Human Projects. SimCoach will leverage these pre-existing projects primarily by making use of infrastructure and art assets for re-use as a platform for creating and evolving research prototypes. This includes the game engine connections and art repositories from the Gunslinger project, as well as Art assets and development tools created in the ELECT, TACQ, SickCall and Virtual Patient projects. The Smartbody project will also provide relevant animation tools. On the clinical front, the existing knowledge base from researchers involved in the PTSD, RERC and VRCPAT projects will be especially relevant for informing conceptual development as they pertain to psychosocial and cognitive-motor issues.

2.4   Government Furnished Equipment (GFE)/Government Furnished Information (GFI) Required

ICT will require access to government personnel for the purpose of understanding the target audience, identifying needs, informing design, and testing the system. Needed personnel will include government social workers, medical professionals, senior leaders (COs and 1SG, BN and BDE CDRs and CSMs), other military personnel with perspective (Chaplains, finance officers), junior leaders (NCOs, PLs), troops (across ranks, services, on-post vs. off-post, mental/physical health afflicted, "healthy") and family members/significant others.

3.0   Schedule

Year 1

Task 1. Conduct target audience research

	GFY09	GFY10										
	Q4	Q1			Q2			Q3			Q4	
	Sep	Oct	Nov	Dec	Jan	Feb	Mar	Apr	May	Jun	Jul	Aug
1.1 Establish teams												
1.2 Establish and execute early focus group plans (PTSD, Depression, Family/Interpersonal issues)												
1.4 Investigate and enhance existing DCoE affiliated web-based content (PTSD, Depression, Family/Interpersonal issues)												
1.5 Dialog development with user-centered consultants to feed production team (PTSD, Depression, Family/Interpersonal issues)												
1.6 Provide user-centered team feedback												

Task 2. Design User Experience

	GFY09	GFY10										
	Q4	Q1			Q2			Q3			Q4	
	Sep	Oct	Nov	Dec	Jan	Feb	Mar	Apr	May	Jun	Jul	Aug
2.1 Design overall user experience												
2.2 Design user interaction with virtual personas												
2.3 Research and development of advanced interaction mgmt.												
2.4 Develop promo video												

Task 3. Content creation

	GFY09	GFY10										
	Q4	Q1			Q2			Q3			Q4	
	Sep	Oct	Nov	Dec	Jan	Feb	Mar	Apr	May	Jun	Jul	Aug
3.1 Design information architecture												
3.2 Content production												

28

Task 4. Development

	GFY09	GFY10										
	Q4	Q1			Q2				Q3		Q4	
	Sep	Oct	Nov	Dec	Jan	Feb	Mar	Apr	May	Jun	Jul	Aug
4.1 Design and develop system architecture												
4.2 Develop components												
4.3 System integration and testing												

Task 5. Assessment

	GFY09	GFY10										
	Q4	Q1			Q2				Q3		Q4	
	Sep	Oct	Nov	Dec	Jan	Feb	Mar	Apr	May	Jun	Jul	Aug
5.1 Design formative evaluation for SimCoach prototype												
5.2 Focus group and individual interviews												

September –November Establish user-centered teams [1.1]
- Focus groups (PTSD, Depression, Family/interpersonal issues): Investigate IRB requirements, define focus groups/individual interviews of interest, plan interviews [1.2.1 -1.2.5]

- Initial analysis of content and delivery of existing DCOE resources [1.4.1-1.4.3, 3.1.1.1, 3.1.1.2]
- Initiate design of information architecture [3.1.1,3.1.2]
- Design overarching messages/themes/experience for users at the site [2.1, 2.2]
- Design system architecture [4.1]
  - o Assess technological feasibility of critical virtual-human components [4.1.1]
  - o Identify planned new components [4.1.1]
  - o Determine information exchange requirements [4.1.2]
- Initiate "Service-ization" of existing core components (NL, Smartbody) [4.1.2, 4.2.2]
- Launch basic web application and infrastructure [4.2.1]
  - o Instantiate basic site features – blog, forums, anonymous contact form to provide feedback/suggestions
- Initiate community design process for input on design of characters/experience [2.1]
  - o Concept art [3.4.1.1]
  - o Example dialogues/complete interactions [3.2.2]
- Identify key personalization needs (understanding that this will be very limited in the first year) [2.3]
- Develop promo video – on-camera interviews with leaders, target audience, examples of possible characters/experience, promotion of community site [2.4]
- Deliver initial synthetic voice with CMU Flite platform [4.2.5.3]
- Initiate research on advanced interaction management [2.3]

December – March

- Focus groups (PTSD, Depression, Family/interpersonal issues): : Final IRB approvals, commence focus group/individual interviews [1.2.9-1.2.11]
- Review progress of DCoE website content analysis [1.4.5]
- Integrate results of focus groups with DCoE web-based content gathering and refinement [1.4.4,1.4.6]
- Initiate virtual human behavior content-creation and pipeline development [3.1.3, 3.1.4, 3.1.5, 4.2.3]
  - o Initiate development of content authoring tools (for internal development-use first) [4.2.3]
  - o Mock-up dialogues with virtual humans (for wizard of oz tests) [3.1.3, 3.2.2]
  - o Formalize triage capability [3.1.4]
  - o Start informal clinical dialog development - user-centered and production team(PTSD/Depression, Family Issues) [1.5.1, 3.1.4]
  - o Prototype initial capability to offline-export SmartBody Animations [4.2.5.2]
- Initiate avatar art development [3.2.2]
  - o Develop drafts/concept art
- Continue design/development of web application components, virtual human components/service-ization [4.2.1, 4.2.2]
- Continue development of web community and resource content [3.1.7]
- Deliver initial advanced face and gesture controller [4.2.5.1]

April– June

- Commence formalized dialog development – user-centered and production team [1.5.2, 3.1.4]
- Incrementally deliver dialog content to production team [1.5.3, 3.1.4]
  - o Deliver basic demographic and history dialog [1.5.3.1]
  - o Deliver PTSD dialog [1.5.3.2]
- Continue content creation and testing [3.2]
  - o Usability tests of dialogue through wizard-of-oz sessions [1.5.2, 3.2.2,5.2]
  - o Begin advice generation modeling [3.2.3]
- Continue avatar development, aesthetic refinement and animation development/testing [3.2.1]
  - o Continue to refine dialogue mock-ups through wizard-of-oz testing
  - o Refine concept art and begin animation tests
- Finalize service/API specifications early in milestone [4.1.2]
  - o Achieve service-level integration (paper-based) across system tiers [4.2.3]
- Continue design/development of web application components [4.2.1]
- Continue design/development of virtual human components (ideally NL is online by now, and portions of the VH (SmartBody) is close so that they can be used in the above tests) [4.2.2]
- Achieve basic integration between web, virtual human and external resource layers (may require stubs/example data) [4.2.1.3]
- Achieve full integration of web-embodied virtual human (animation, dialogue, NL) [4.2.3]
- Deliver two additional synthetic voices with CMU Flite platform [4.2.5.3]
- Focus group and individual interviews on SimCoach prototype [5.2]

July– August
- Incrementally deliver dialog content to production team [1.5.3, 3.1.4]
  - o Deliver Depression dialog [1.5.3.3]
  - o Deliver Family and Interpersonal issues dialog to production team [1.5.3.4]
- System level integration and testing (web application / virtual human / external resources) [4.3]
- Finalize content development (behavior, domain models) [3.2.2, 3.2.3, 4.2.4]
- Conduct controlled testing/QA with full system [4.3, 1.3]
- End of May/Year 1: Delivery of working alpha (it runs, has been tested in controlled user tests, parts may still be buggy (highest risks: latency, animations, natural language) [4.3]
- Examine and review SimCoach Version 1 prototype by user-centered team [1.6.1]
- Focus group and individual interviews on SimCoach prototype [5.2]
- Design strategy and methodology for formative evaluation of SimCoach Prototype 1 (PTSD/Depression/Family/Interpersonal issues) [5.1]

Year 2

Task 1. Conduct target audience research

	GFY10	GFY11										
	Q4	Q1			Q2			Q3			Q4	
	Sep	Oct	Nov	Dec	Jan	Feb	Mar	Apr	May	Jun	Jul	Aug
1.3 Establish and execute focus group plan (TBI/Addictions domain)												
1.4 Investigate and enhance existing DCoE affiliated web-based content (TBI/Addictions)												
1.5 Dialog development with user-centered consultants to feed production team (TBI/Addictions)												
1.6 Provide user-centered team feedback												

Task 2. Design User Experience

	GFY10	GFY11										
	Q4	Q1			Q2			Q3			Q4	
	Sep	Oct	Nov	Dec	Jan	Feb	Mar	Apr	May	Jun	Jul	Aug
2.1 Design overall user experience												
2.2 Design user interaction with virtual personas												
2.3 Research and development of advanced interaction mgmt.												
2.3 Develop promo video												

Task 3. Content creation

	GFY10	GFY11										
	Q4	Q1			Q2			Q3			Q4	
	Sep	Oct	Nov	Dec	Jan	Feb	Mar	Apr	May	Jun	Jul	Aug
3.1 Design information architecture												
3.2 Content production												

Task 4. Development

	GFY10	GFY11										
	Q4	Q1			Q2			Q3			Q4	
	Sep	Oct	Nov	Dec	Jan	Feb	Mar	Apr	May	Jun	Jul	Aug
4.1 Develop system architecture												
4.2 Develop components												
4.3 System integration and testing												

Task 5. Assessment

	GFY10	GFY11										
	Q4	Q1			Q2			Q3			Q4	
	Sep	Oct	Nov	Dec	Jan	Feb	Mar	Apr	May	Jun	Jul	Aug
5.3 Conduct formative user testing with prototype 1 system for design/development support												
5.4 Compile and analyze data from formative evaluation results and report on results												
5.5 Design summative evaluation methodology for SimCoach prototype 1												
Conduct effectiveness assessment of PTSD, Depression and Family/Interpersonal issues module												

September-October
- Rollout of working alpha for testing [4.2.1, 4.2.2]
- Continuing testing/QA [4.3]
- Delivery/launch of working beta [4.2.1, 4.2.2]
- Focus groups (TBI/Addictions): Review group/individual interviews, compile interview data and distribute to team [1.3.1-1.3.2]
- Design and development of content-creation and pipeline tools for end-user authoring [3.1, 4.2.3]
- Commence development of TBI and Addiction module content [1.5.4]
- Identify priorities for new features/characters/content [2.1, 2.2]
- Ongoing site/content maintenance [3.2]
- Research emotional/stylistic speech synthesis techniques [4.2.5.3]
- Conduct formative user testing with prototype 1 system for design/development support [5.3]

–November-January
- Testing/QA [4.3]
- Begin design of new features/accompanying infrastructure – especially refinements to personalization and authoring? [2.1, 2.2, 4.2]
- Commence informal TBI/Addictions dialog development with user-centered consultations [1.5.5]
- Commence formalized development of TBI/Addictions dialog options [1.5.6]
- Ongoing site/content maintenance [3.2]
- Design formative and summative evaluation methodology for TBI/Additions prototype [1.3.3]

- Compile and analyze data from formative evluation results and report on results [5.4]

February – August
- Incrementally deliver dialog content to production team [1.5.7]
    o Deliver TBI dialog
    o Deliver Addictions dialog
- Design summative evaluation methodology for SimCoach prototype 1 (PTSD, Depression, Family/interpersonal issues module) [5.5]
- Conduct effectiveness assessment of PTSD, Depression, Family/interpersonal issues module [5.6]
- Regular pushes of refinements to front-end [4.2,4.3]
- End of May/Year 2: Delivery of working beta of authoring tools and/or APIs
- Examine and review SimCoach TBI/Addictions prototype by user-centered team [1.6.2]
- Ongoing site/content maintenance [3.2]
- Deliver synthetic voices with improved emotion/style control [4.2.5.3]

Project Milestones

- Promotional video of the concept and future vision
    - Delivery: 3 months after contract start
- Website where SimCoach and other resources can be accessed
    - Delivery: First launch within 3 months after contract start
    - Delivery: Regular revisions as appropriate throughout period of performance
- Working alpha of virtual humans (it runs, has been tested in controlled user tests, parts may still be buggy (highest risks: latency, animations, natural language) that will support rigorous testing. There will be at least two interactive virtual humans (male and female). The specific interaction will have to be defined as part of the design process leading up to milestone 1 but it is expected to include the capabilities for gathering basic demographic information to help identify the problems, engaging in supportive dialog, and helping to connect the user to health content and regional healthcare providers. Some kind of personalization will be available. The content will include an emphasis on PTSD/Depression and on family/general wellness issues. The user will also have some limited opportunities for voice input.
    - Delivery: 12 months after contract start
- Report about assessments with working alpha
- Revised/QA-ed working beta virtual humans for general launch
    - Delivery: 14 months after contract start
- Virtual humans with refinements/additional capabilities based on feedback from user testing. The virtual humans will also have a richer model of the user to allow for deeper personalization and tailoring of the experience. The virtual human characters will extend their focus to traumatic brain injury (TBI) and addiction.
    - Delivery: 24 months after contract start
- Initial authoring tool and APIs to allow 3rd party clinicians to author SimCoach questions and responses (created in Year 1) and otherwise leverage the existing content and infrastructure
    - Delivery: 24 months after contract start

4.0   INTELLECTUAL PROPERTY & LICENSING RIGHTS

4.1   USC Intellectual Property

As per the ICT basic contract.

5.0   APPENDICES

5.1   Appendix A - Budget Justifications

Travel
A critical aspect of the proposed research progress is the need to disseminate results and obtain timely feedback from the broader scientific community through participation in national and international meetings. Maintaining ICT's leadership roles in these events provides visibility and broader impact of these projects. The proposed budget covers travel by the lead researchers and graduate students to several major conferences, as well as local mileage to travel to focus group facilities in San Diego, CA. In addition, the proposed budget covers travel to attend interim progress report meetings with the customer. We have also budgeted funds to support the ICT's production team travel to various military installations for focus group studies and testing. Lastly, we have allocated up to $2,000 per year for domestic travel for consultants for interim progress meetings and collaboration either at the ICT in Marina del Rey, to collaborate with other consultants, or with the customer.

Equipment
Servers: The budget includes two primary servers for both web application hosting and computational support of the virtual human processes. We require a scalable system (i.e. rack) to adjust to our end user needs for what will be a computational intense virtual human application for simultaneous web sessions.

Materials and Supplies (M&S)
M&S Burn Rate: The ICT Materials and supplies burn rate normally includes items that are less than $500 and are not identified in the budgets as discreet supplies.

Workstations: Several workstations are budgeted for development work to support planned hires and/or replace workstations for other project staff.

Subject fees are proposed to assess the validity of the emotion model. Subjects are estimated at $20 per subject, for 175 subjects ($3,500 total).

Software Licenses: The proposed budget includes software licenses such as VMWare, Adobe Acrobat, dialogue system development and testing (specific software needs will be determined based on further evaluation of actual project needs)

Laptop, site services and supplies: The USC School of Social work has budgeted for laptop, site services, and supplies and refreshments for user centered evaluations within the Camp Pendleton site. Social Work will conduct eight focus group sessions per month, at an estimated cost of $250 per month to cover the cost of printed materials and refreshments. Typically focus group participants receive monetary compensation for their participation; however, participants for these focus groups will receive refreshments for volunteering their time.

Facility fees: The School of Social work budget includes the cost to lease commerial office space in San Diego, CA for conducting focus groups. This space is estimated at $1,667 for two office spaces plus the cost of internet, phone and fax.

Consultants

Expert consultation is required for the clinical design, development and iterative evaluation of the SimCoach modules/vignettes (e.g., PTSD, Depression, Family Issues, TBI and Addiction) and implementation strategies that will lead to the creation of a "gateway" site for psychological disorder and TBI healthcare information dissemination for military personnel, veterans and their families. The site will be inhabited by a selection of varied Virtual Human agents that will engage in some level of dialog with the users and help provide guidance for information resources, access to care and other relevant information. The proposed budget includes the following consultants:

Barbara Rothbaum

Dr. Rothbaum will help create and evaluate content for the PTSD and psychiatric symptoms modules. She will also contribute to the conceptualization of the virtual humans. She will help write dialogue between the virtual humans and users in the areas of overcoming treatment barriers and the evaluation and treatment of PTSD and related disorders.

JoAnn Difede

Dr. Difede will help create and evaluate content for the PTSD and psychiatric symptoms modules. She will also contribute to the conceptualization of the virtual humans. She will help write dialogue between the virtual humans and users in the areas of overcoming treatment barriers and the evaluation and treatment of PTSD and related disorders.

Patrick Bordnick

As a licensed social worker, Dr. Bordnick will provide expertise on the role of clinical social work practice with individual and families targeted toward warfighters and their families. He also has international recognition in the area of technology applications for the treatment of addictive behaviors. Specific activities will also include: assist in content creation and feedback on mental health disorders and interpersonal issues generally and will lead the effort for the addictions module. He will also bring further expertise in the areas of social work assessments and case management, dialog development, and review of prototypes. His research background will also provide assets for the user-centered evaluation that will take place during this project.

Ben Lok

Dr. Lok will provide guidance on the development of virtual human technologies, leveraging experience of integrating virtual humans into medical school curriculums, public exhibits and clinic. Will provide guidance on ways that interaction with virtual humans can be guided to support clinical aims

Kristine Nowak

Dr. Nowak will assist with dialog and avatar design and creation to help the SimCoach be able to conduct a useful interaction with the user. Dr. Nowak has training in the evaluation of avatars for different uses across contexts and an understanding of how to best present information to people using different modalities (text, audio, visual, etc). Dr. Nowak will make recommendations for features and types of avatars that would best be utilized for different contexts with different audiences, and advise on the protocols followed in the usability analysis of the system.

Raymond Scurfield

Dr. Scurfield is the Director of the Katrina Research Center, a veteran and a Social worker with a long history in the area of PTSD and psychsocial reactions to trauma. He is also an expert in Internet resources for these same topics. He will provide expertise on the role of clinical social work practice with individual and families targeted toward warfighters and their families. Specific activities will also include: assist in content creation and feedback on mental health disorders and interpersonal issues generally and will also bring further expertise in the areas of social work assessments and case management, dialog development, and review of prototypes.

Physical Therapy Consultant (year two)

The Physical Therapy consultant will help create and evaluate content for the TBI Module in year 2. The consultant will contribute to the conceptualization of Simcoach virtual humans as they are relevant to provide advice and direct users to content relevant for physical therapy and motor rehabilitation issues following TBI (and also prosthetics issues). This person will help write dialogue between the virtual humans and users in the areas of overcoming treatment barriers and the evaluation and treatment of sensorimotor impairments due to TBI. The specific individual for this consultancy has not been identified yet.

Subcontracts

National Center for PTSD - Josef Ruzek and Laurie Sloane

Drs. Ruzek and Sloane will provide unique expertise via their positions within the National Center For PTSD. The NCPSTD has a long history of development of internet content addressing PTSD and their input will bring that essential content into the SimCoach project. They will help create and evaluate content for the PTSD and psychiatric symptoms modules. Dr. Sloane was the NCPSTD developer of the online interactive resource, "Returning from the War Zone: Guide for Families" and will add expertise in the family and significant others domain of SimCoach. They will also contribute to the conceptualization of the virtual humans and assist in creating dialogue between the virtual humans and users in the areas of overcoming treatment barriers and the evaluation and treatment of PTSD and related disorders.

Interaction Designers

This contract will fund an external design and content production team responsible primarily for virtual character production process. Tasks include character concept and design, dialogue authoring, behavioral modeling, usability and other user testing.

Video Production

This contract will be used for production of promotional trailer to support SimCoach effort. Costs to contractor include all pre-and post- production costs and all filming costs.

Carnegie Mellon University (CMU)
Under the direction of Alan Black, Associate Professor, CMU will design, record, build and tune at least 3 synthetic voices suitable for the target application.

5.2   Appendix B - References

[1] Bilmes, L. (2007). Soldiers Returning from Iraq and Afghanistan: The Long-term Costs of Providing Veterans Medical Care and Disability Benefits, Faculty Research Working Paper Series, John F. Kennedy School of Government - Harvard University. Downloaded on 1/20/2007 at: http://ksgnotes1.harvard.edu/Research/wpaper.nsf/rwp/RWP07-001

[2] Jelinek, P. & Hefling, K. (2009). AP Report: Army suicides at record high, passing civilians. Downloaded on 1/29/2009 at: http://www.google.com/hostednews/ap/article/ALeqM5jrRijfpxg8ZdUbcDpGbmnEpYPH9w D9616BB80

[3] DOD Mental Health Task Force Report. (2007). Downloaded on 6/15/2007 at: http://www.health.mil/dhb/mhtf/MHTF-Report-Final.pdf

[4] Institute of Medicine of the Academies of Science. (2007). Treatment of PTSD: An Assessment of the Evidence. Downloaded on 10/18/2007 at: http://www.nap.edu/catalog.php?record_id=11955#toc

[5] Dole-Shalala Commission. (2007). Serve, Support, Simplify: Report of the President's Commission on Care for America's Returning Wounded Warriors.

[6] Tanielian, T., Jaycox, L.H,, Schell, T.L., Marshall, G.N., Burnam, M.A., Eibner, C., Karney, B.R., Meredith, L.S., Ringel, J.S., Vaiana, M.E., et al. (2008). Invisible Wounds of War: Summary and Recommendations for Addressing Psychological and Cognitive Injuries. *Rand Report* Retrieved 04/18/2008, from: http://veterans.rand.org/

[7] American Psychological Association Presidential Task Force on Military Deployment Services for Youth, Families and Service Members. (2007). The Psychological Needs of U.S. Military Service Members and Their Families: A Preliminary Report. Retrieved 04/18/2007, from: http://www.apa.org/releases/MilitaryDeploymentTaskForceReport.pdf

[8] Annon, J. (1976). Behavioral Treatment of Sexual Problems. Harper-Collins. NY, NY.

[9] Bickmore, T., Pfeifer, L., and Jack, B. (2009) Taking the Time to Care: Empowering Low Health Literacy Hospital Patients with Virtual Nurse Agents *Proceedings of the ACM SIGCHI Conference on Human Factors in Computing Systems (CHI)*, Boston, MA.

[10] Bickmore, T., Pfeifer, L., and Paasche-Orlow, M. (to appear) Using Computer Agents to Explain Medical Documents to Patients with Low Health Literacy *Patient Education and Counseling.*

[11] Weisband, S. and Kiesler, S. (1996). Self disclosure on computer forms: meta-analysis and implications. In *Proceedings of the SIGCHI Conference on Human Factors in Computing*

Systems: Common Ground (Vancouver, British Columbia, Canada, April 13 - 18, 1996). M. J. Tauber, Ed. CHI '96. ACM, New York, NY, 3-10.

[12] Shneiderman, B. (2000). The limits of speech recognition. *Commun. ACM* 43, 9 (Sept.), 63-65.

[13] Baylor, A., Kim, S. (2008). The Effects of Agent Nonverbal Communication on Procedural and Attitudinal Learning Outcomes. *IVA 2008*: 208-214.

[14] Gratch, J. Okhmatovskaia, A., Lamothe, F., Marsella, S., Morales, M., van der Werf, R.J., Morency, L-P. (2006). Virtual Rapport. *IVA 2006*: 14-27.

[15] Van Vugt, H. (2008). Embodied Agents from a user's perspective. Faculty of Social Sciences Dissertation, VU University of Amsterdam, 2008.

[16] Marsella, S., Johnson,W.L., and LaBore, C. (2000). *Interactive pedagogical drama.* Fourth International Conference on Autonomous Agents, Montreal, Canada.

[17] Marsella, S., Johnson,W.L., and LaBore, C. (2003). *Interactive pedagogical drama for health interventions.* Conference on Artificial intelligence in Education, Sydney, Australia.

PART II – STATEMENT OF WORK (SOW)

1.0 Scope

The SimCoach project is focused on attracting and engaging Warfighters and their significant others who might not otherwise seek help (whether due to stigma, lack of awareness or a general reluctance to seek help). The goal will be to create an experience that will motivate these Warfighters and their significant others to take the first step – to empower themselves with regard to their healthcare (e.g., psychological health and traumatic brain injury) and general personal welfare (i.e., other non-medical stressors such as economic or relationship issues) – and encourage them to take the next step towards seeking other, more formal resources that are available.

The project will be a collaboration between treatment and service providers, designers and developers of immersive technologies, and military personnel. The project will integrate virtual human technologies with off-the-shelf systems and other available research technologies. The result will be an easy-to-access platform that will be extensible by others as needed/desired.

This project shall be delivered to the Defense Centers of Excellence for Psychological Health and Traumatic Brain Injury.

1.1 Objective

The SimCoach project is focused on attracting and engaging Warfighters and their significant others who might not otherwise seek help (whether due to stigma, lack of awareness or a general reluctance to seek help). The goal will be to create an experience that will motivate these Warfighters and their significant others to take the first step – to empower themselves with regard to their healthcare (e.g., psychological health and traumatic brain injury) and general personal welfare (i.e., other non-medical stressors such as economic or relationship issues) – and encourage them to take the next step towards seeking other, more formal resources that are available.

The result shall be a system that is widely accessible and allows users to remain completely anonymous. The design and content will be based on a collaboration between treatment and service providers, designers and developers of immersive technologies, and military personnel. It will take into consideration substantial input from the target user community.

1.2 Background

Within the military population (which includes both warfighters and warfighter families), the need for healthcare information is growing at an astounding rate. In spite of a Herculean effort on the part of the DOD to produce and disseminate behavioral health programs for military personnel and their families, the complexity of the issues involved continue to challenge the best efforts of military mental health care experts, administrators and providers. Since 2004, numerous blue ribbon panels of experts have attempted to assess the current DOD and VA healthcare delivery system and provide recommendations for improvement. Most of these reports cite a need for identification and implementation of ways to enhance the healthcare dissemination/delivery system for military personnel and their families in a fashion that provides better awareness and access to care while reducing the stigma of help-seeking. In essence, new methods are required to reduce barriers to care.

The intention of the SimCoach project is to leverage a variety of techniques to design the user experience. One source of knowledge is the medical/clinical practice. One potentially relevant clinical model is the PLISSIT clinical framework (**P**ermission, **L**imited **I**nformation, **S**pecific **S**uggestions, and **I**ntensive **T**herapy [8]), which provides an established model for encouraging help-seeking behaviors in persons who may feel stigma and insecurity regarding their condition. In the SimCoach project, we would likely only be able to address the "PLISS" components, leaving the intensive therapy component to live professionals that users could be referred to. Another potentially relevant model is the Trans-theoretical Model of Behavioral Change: (1) Pre-contemplation, (2) Contemplation, (3) Preparation, (4) Action, (5) Maintenance, (6) Termination. In this model, a person can be taken from stage 1 to stage 2 through consciousness raising, from stage 2 to stage 3 through self-reevaluation, and from stage 3 to stage 4 through lowering barriers.

Another source of knowledge is the social work practice. These models take a case management approach, serving as an advocate and guide. Social work input will be garnered via our collaboration with the USC School of Social Work and with internationally respected outside consultants. Finally, another source of knowledge is the entertainment/game practice. This community is not typically oriented towards healthcare. However, their models focus most explicitly on attracting and engaging individuals that can inform the design of a more friendly or otherwise appealing experience – to help get people "in the door." Entertainment and marketing techniques for engaging and/or influencing behavior include creating an experience that will result in the suspension of disbelief, "hooks" that motivate people to keep trying, and well-crafted messaging/experience that lead to a consistency that could lead to additional opportunities to retain the user.

1.3 Special Considerations

1.3.1 Security Classification

This effort is UNCLASSIFIED. No classified or access to classified material will be involved in the performance of this effort.

1.3.2 Information Restrictions

Fundamental research, as defined by National Security Decision Directive 189, the Export Administration Regulations ("EAR"; 15 CFR parts 730-774) and the International Traffic in Arms Regulations ("ITAR"; 22 CFR parts 120-130), means basic and applied research in science and engineering, the results of which ordinarily are published and shared broadly within the scientific community. This is distinguished from proprietary research and from industrial development, design, production, and product utilization, the results of which ordinarily are restricted for proprietary or national security reasons.

The parties consider the work required by this contract to be fundamental research. The Contractor may freely publish, present, and share any information associated with this effort without restriction.

For purposes of this effort, export-controlled information and technology means information and technology subject to export controls established in the EAR and the ITAR. Export-controlled information and technology may include "Government Furnished Restricted Information," which shall mean any documents, electronic media or oral information explicitly identified by the Government as being Controlled Unclassified Information (CUI), Sensitive But Unclassified (SBU) Information, or For Official Use Only (FOUO) Information.

The parties do not anticipate that in performance of this contract the Contractor will generate or need access to export-controlled information or technology, or any Government Furnished Restricted Information. If, during performance of this contract, the Government or the Contractor becomes aware that the Contractor will generate or need access to export-controlled information or technology or Government Furnished restricted information, it shall notify the other party. The parties shall then jointly either—
(1) Negotiate a contract modification to specifically identify any such export-controlled information or technology or Government Furnished Restricted Information and to identify any specific controls and publication restrictions applicable to such information;
(2) Negotiate a contract modification that eliminates the requirement for performance of work that would involve export-controlled information or technology or Government Furnished Restricted Information; or
(3) Negotiate the transfer of non-restricted information that would allow Contractor to fulfill its obligations under this contract.
It shall be the Government's responsibility to identify such Government Furnished Restricted Information prior to release to the ICT by marking all restricted documents and electronic media with the applicable Government designation or by explicitly notifying the ICT of any such restrictions applicable to information conveyed in the course of meetings, telephone conferences or other oral discussions relating to this effort. To aid the Government in performing its responsibility, when the ICT seeks or receives information for the first time (whether in person, by phone, or otherwise) from Government personnel or government contractor personnel who have not previously been involved with the ICT on this project, the ICT will endeavor to remind them that information provided to the ICT is not restricted unless restrictions are identified and agreed upon in advance in the manner prescribed in this agreement.

In the event that the export controlled information involved in the contract is limited to Government Furnished Restricted Information (i.e., the Contractor will not generate any export-controlled information), any publication restrictions agreed to by the parties shall be limited to a pre-publication review requirement solely for the purpose of ensuring that the Government Furnished Restricted Information is not disclosed. The acceptance of such a limited pre-publication review requirement shall not alter the status of the research as Fundamental Research or otherwise inhibit the right of the Contractor to publish the results of its research.

1.3.3 Personnel Restrictions

There are no restrictions on the participation of non-U.S. Persons in this effort, except that ICT shall not provide Non-U.S. Persons with access to Government Furnished Restricted Information without prior written approval from the ICT Government Program Manager or other designated Government representative (unless they meet the specific requirements for an International Traffic in Arms Regulations (ITAR) license exemption). For purposes of this effort, the term "Non-U.S. Persons" shall mean any individual other than a U.S. citizen, a legal permanent resident ("Green Card" holder), or a legal political asylee or refugee.

1.3.4 Equipment

N/A

2.0 Applicable Documents

Annon, J. (1976). Behavioral Treatment of Sexual Problems. Harper-Collins. NY, NY.

3.0 Tasks/Technical Requirements

In order to accomplish the objectives identified above, ICT shall accomplish the following tasks.

1. ICT shall have a user-centered team to conduct target audience research, vet DCoE target resources, and provide input to content-creation process.

The approach shall include
- Establishing the design and SME teams
- Conducting focus group tests
- Filling any needed gaps in web-based content
- Developing dialogue in the areas of PTSD and TBI
- Iterate on dialogue based on feedback

2. ICT shall research and design user experience.

The approach shall include:
- Designing overall user experience
- Designing user interaction with virtual personas
- Researching, development and assessment of advanced interaction management
- Developing promotional video and other complementary materials for communicating need and vision to decision-makers, people who can provide input, and other stakeholders

3. ICT shall create content.

The approach shall include:
- Designing information architecture (oriented towards service-oriented architecture model)
- Content production including virtual human avatar models, virtual human dialogue content and behavior models, and static clinical content to populate the online repository.

4. ICT shall develop the SimCoach system.

Broadly, the approach shall include:

- Developing system architecture (oriented towards service-oriented architecture model)
- Developing system components including web application, content pipeline and authoring tools, web-based administration tools, and virtual human subsystem
- System integration and testing

5. ICT shall conduct assessments.

The approach shall include:

- Design strategy and methodology for formative evaluation of SimCoach Prototype 1 (PTSD/Depression/Family and Interpersonal issues)
- Focus group and individual interviews
- Conduct Formative user testing with Prototype 1 system for design/development support
- Compile and analyze data from Formative evaluation results and report on results for improving next prototype (Months 17-18).
- Design Summative evaluation methodology for SimCoach Prototype 1 (PTSD, Depression, Family and Interpersonal issues modules)
- Conduct effectiveness assessment (or Summative Evaluation) of PTSD, Depression and Family and Interpersonal Issues Module
- Conduct Formative and Summative evaluation of TBI/Addictions Module in YEAR 3

Deliverables:

- Promotional video of the concept and future vision
- Website where SimCoach and other resources can be accessed
- Working alpha of virtual humans
- Report about assessments with working alpha
- Revised/QA-ed working beta virtual humans for general launch
- Virtual humans with refinements/additional capabilities based on feedback from user testing.
- Initial authoring tool and APIs to allow 3rd party clinicians to author SimCoach questions and responses and otherwise leverage the existing content and infrastructure

At month six, a design document with more detailed specification of the system will be produced for review by the customer. The design document will describe the system to be delivered at the end of twelve months after contract start and as much detail as possible for year 2. Due to the novelty, size, scope and unknowable issues (at the current time) that are relevant to this project (results from early focus groups and individual user feedback trials, exploration of solutions for potential technical integration challenges, advances in voice recognition, etc.), we require this time period during the starting phase of the project to generate a more detailed and prioritized summary of user requirements, the results of which will feed the system concept (use cases, etc.). During the time leading up to this point we will determine what system features optimally meet the needs of the users and are technically feasible. This will allow ICT and the customer to have a documented record of what has been specifically agreed upon at that time. After user tests at the beginning of year 2, the design document will be updated to reflect the additional input as appropriate. This will insure that in the end we will build something that everybody truly wants and can use, rather than rigidly adhering to an initial plan that later user-centered findings advise against. The introduction of this design phase will not significantly delay any of the development tasks.

Personnel - Task Level Technical Coordinator (TLTC)

CDR Russell Shilling, Scientific Advisor - Psychological Health Defense Center of Excellence for Psychological Health and Traumatic Brain Injury, will function as the designated TLTC for the purpose of project coordination. Any potential changes in tasks, deliverables, or scope of effort, or any potential changes which may impact contract costs, will be brought to the attention of RDECOM-STTC ICT Contracting Officer's Representative (COR), Mr. Joe Brennan, who will, if agreed upon, perform the coordination required to enable the ICT to execute the changes. The final approval authority for all project deliverables will be the ICT Program Manager, Mr. John Hart.

SimCoach Onsite Evaluation: Preliminary Results

This appendix contains slides describing preliminary results of SimCoach user testing, which the SimCoach development team provided to the authors at the beginning of the evaluation.

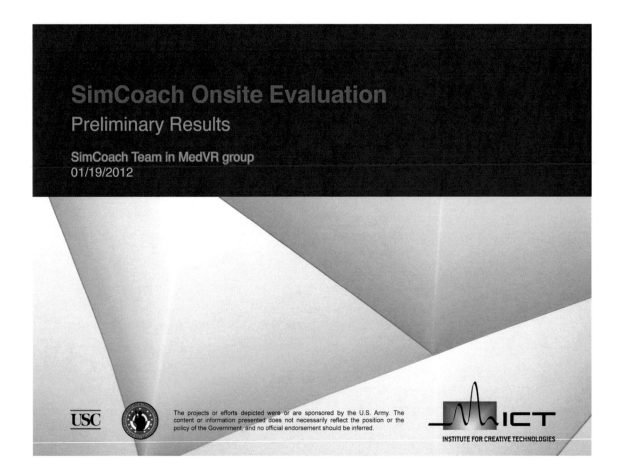

Overview

- **Introduction** (Methodology)

- **Demographics**

- **Results and Problems** (Summary of Users' Feedback)

- **Suggestions of Updates**

- **Further Work**

Introduction

- Iterative evaluation cycles over course of development

- Between July and December 2011, a total of 111 participants took part in user testing sessions. Participants were invited to take part in the testing if they were over the age of 18 and were an Active Military Service Member, Veteran or family member of a Service Member or Veteran.

- The participants were asked to complete a demographic survey before interacting with the SimCoach character Bill Ford. Following the interaction, participants completed a post-interaction survey and structured interview.

- The mean age of participants was 41 years old (range 18 – 76 years old). Majority of the participants were the Discharged (60%, n = 62) and members of the US Army (61%, n = 68).

- A total of 88 participants completed the post interaction surveys.

- Overall the response to the interaction with the SimCoach character were positive. The majority the users felt SimCoach could be successful because of anonymity, confidentiality, and objectivity. The negative comments about the system were often the result of the user becoming frustrated with Bill' s delayed or inappropriate responses.

USC

ICT
INSTITUTE FOR CREATIVE TECHNOLOGIES

Demographics (1)

- **Test Sites**

Location	Dates	Sample	N
College of the Canyons	07/26 – 27, 08/03	Students with military background, some were family members	9
Volunteers of America Los Angeles	07/28, 08/04	Younger Veterans	7
US Vets Long Beach	08/26	Veterans, some Active Duty	6
Joint Military Pacific Command	10/19	Active Duty, recently deployed	4
USC San Diego Academic Center:	11/17	Students with military background, some were family members	4
Naomi House	12/02	Unemployed, as a result, homeless. Have issues with mental health and substance abuse	5
California National Guard	12/03	Active Duty, recently deployed	24
Salvation Army	12/09	Unemployed, as a result, homeless. Have issues with mental health and substance abuse	19

Demographics (2)

- **Gender**

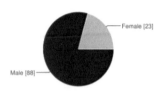

- **Age**

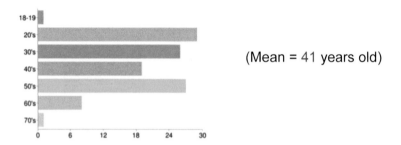

(Mean = 41 years old)

Demographics (3)

- **Current military status**

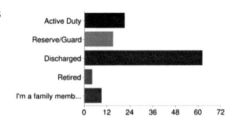

- **Branch of service**

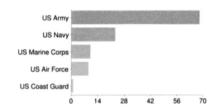

Demographics (4): Participant Issues and Challenges

- Sample characteristics
  - All volunteer samples of convenience
  - Response Bias: some subjects didn't have any issue to talk about
  - Social Psych Factors: subjects observed during interaction
  - Varied Sample: Salvation Army and Naomi House sample had many users who were unemployed and often homeless. Thus, most of the Veteran participants in this group had issues with mental health and substance abuse However, no data available for statistical assessment of the impact of this issue.

General Feedback about the SimCoach

- "Objectivity, Confidentiality, Anonymity, Unlimited time and interaction, Ease of accessibility" (VA003 & MSC001)

- "It feels easier to "talk" someone rather than to just try to do searches that are often not relevant to what your search terms are and more comfortable than just picking options from drop down menus and way better than using a telephone tree." (SCUSVLB16)

- "I found it easier to speak to Bill than a human being." (SCUSVLB19)

- "This is awesome, a little more work on the fluidity of the program and the responsiveness of the avatar and I feel this program will be very successful. Great job." (SDAC3)

Questionnaire Results & Problems

Results: System

- **Responsiveness of system**

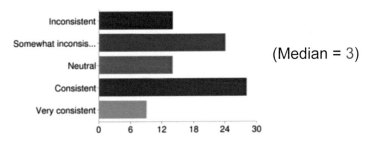

(Median = 3)

(1=inconsistent 2=somewhat inconsistent 3=neutral 4=consistent 5=very consistent)

> These inconsistencies could be the result of the different types of questions participants asked, the language they used and the internet connection. Further analysis is required.

Challenges: Consistent responsiveness of System

- **Responsiveness of system**
  :Somewhat inconsistent

  - "Sometimes the audio script is run together at an unnatural speed." (SCUSVLB16)
  - "Make Bill's responses quicker. If you start talking about something else, Bill needs to stop talking and go on to the next response." (SDAC1)
  - "This is a nice little tool depending on the individual, not recommended for people with anger issues." (SCUSVLB17), "too slow in responding to a frantic user" (VA004)
  - "The glitches in some inappropriate responses distracted me from developing a "rapport."" (VA014)

Results: Program Stimulation/Flexibility

- **Feeling about the program**
  - Neutral -> Stimulating
  - Flexible -> Somewhat rigid

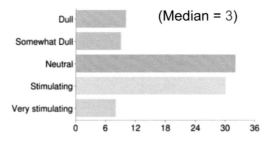

(Median = 3)

(1=dull 2=somewhat dull 3=neutral 4=stimulating 5=very stimulating)

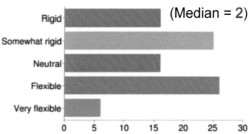

(Median = 2)

(1=rigid 2=somewhat rigid 3=neutral 4=flexible 5=very flexible)

> Further information was gathered about participant's feelings toward the program within the structured interview questions.

> These inconsistencies could be the result of the difference in computer experience and knowledge and/or the wide spread of ages of participants.

12 USC   ICT
INSTITUTE FOR CREATIVE TECHNOLOGIES

Results: Functionality

- **Functionality**
  - It has all the functions and capabilities that I expected: Undecided -> Agree
  - The information provided was effective in helping me plan my next step: Undecided / Agree

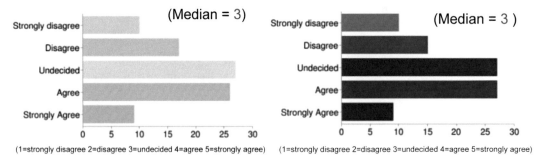

(Median = 3)   (Median = 3)

(1=strongly disagree 2=disagree 3=undecided 4=agree 5=strongly agree)   (1=strongly disagree 2=disagree 3=undecided 4=agree 5=strongly agree)

> Note: participants recruited for these testing sessions were not required to discuss their own issues. Participants did not have to have symptoms of PTSD or depression to take part in testing.

13 USC   INSTITUTE FOR CREATIVE TECHNOLOGIES

Challenges: Flexibility and Diversity of Content

- **Program**
  - **: Somewhat rigid**
  - **: Information was not enough to be effective in helping users plan their next step**

    - "However, when I asked a question about PTSD being related to memory loss I was unable to get an answer." (VOALA11)
    - "there was supposed to be a link, but it never showed up and then the conversation ended." (VOALA 13)
    - "not enough time to answer the questions or comments." (SCUSVLB11)
    - "I have non-combat PTSD that was caused by emotional torment by other soldiers ......" (SCUSVLB16)
    - "The responses to questions are too generic...I don't think that expletives are needed to bond." (SCUSVLB20)
    - "The Simcoach started by taking too much time to build rapport with me....(e.g., barbecuing, or Hawaii)." (SDAC3)
    - "I asked a question about marriage issues, did not address, started asking about me and my mental health." (VA016)
    - "Most of the interaction with Bill seemed geared toward the military member more so than toward the family member. " (MSC001)
    - "I would like to have seen bill not ask so many questions so fast i could not, keep up...." (COC7)

ICT
INSTITUTE FOR CREATIVE TECHNOLOGIES

Results: Character Interaction

- **Interaction with Bill**
    - I understand my issue much better after my interaction w/ the character: Undecided
    - He really knew what I was thinking: Undecided
    - He responded to my thoughts and questions very thoroughly: Agree -> Disagree -> Undecided

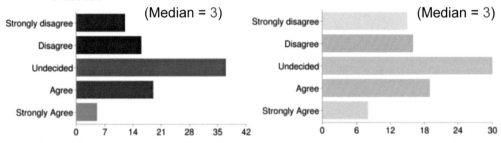

(1=strongly disagree 2=disagree 3=undecided 4=agree 5=strongly agree)   (1=strongly disagree 2=disagree 3=undecided 4=agree 5=strongly agree)

- ➢ Note: participants recruited for these testing sessions were not required to discuss their own issues. Participants did not have to have symptoms of PTSD or depression to take part in testing.

Results: Character Interaction

- **Examples of Bill's ability to carry a conversation (VA interview)**

- Bill seems to lack the ability to put into context certain words, phrases, i.e. "let's go" (meaning let's get going).

- One user pointed out he felt Bill was unable to understand "I've been busy" as it related to being on three deployments.

- One user did not realize that Bill's inquiry into his weight change was used to screen for depression and taken out of context, i.e. being on leave led to eating more and decreased activity = weight gain and not a result of depression.

- At one point, when a user and Bill got more into the conversation, Bill said it was helpful to talk to someone and so the user wrote, "who should I talk too?" Bill said, "avoidance is not the answer." The response didn't match the user's question even though he phrased it as simply as he could. But, Bill's response was really off.

Challenges: Realistic Character

- **Interaction with Bill**
  - **: No good understanding capability for users' complicated answers**
  - **: Didn't respond to my thoughts and questions very thoroughly**

  - "sometimes the preprogrammed responses would show up before i submitted my question or response....many times I would respond and the program said it couldn't understand what I was saying." (COC3)
  - "Bill is good don't like the other sim coaches" (SCUSVLB2) **<- due to "in uniform"?**
  - "Bill doesn't understand complex answers. Bill is a little rigid in what he can respond to." (SCUSVLB16).
  - "Bill's vocabulary was very limited" (SCUSVLB18)
  - "He was a man and I would of felt more comfortable if he was my ethnic....." (SCUSVLB23)
  - "In the beginning the interaction with Bill was completely off. I would ask him about his military experience and he just kept talking about Hawaii. I didn't like that." (COC9: 28 years old & VOALA9, COC2: 20 years old, SCUSVLB16: 53 years old)
  - "Inconsiderate and selfish" , "needs to be more thoughtful or why would we waste our time to someone who has not a sense of feelings." (VOALA15)

Summary of Users' Feedback

- ## Consistent issues
  - Interrupted the user before he finishes typing up a response or watches a video
  - Lacks the ability to put into context certain words or military phrases (military acronym/jargon vocabulary)
  - Lag in response to users' answers
  - It was not always clear how to interact with Bill (e.g. how to word the questions in order for Bill to respond)
  - Took long time to create rapport with users (e.g., barbecuing, or Hawaii)

- ## Contradictory issues
  - **BBQ video**
    - *Pro:* "cool" (Vet Center interview, 25-30 years old)
    - *Con:* "weird question like about the BBQ", "useless" (COC & VOALA: 20-28 years old; SCUSVLB16: 53 years old)
  - **Multiple choice**
    - *Pro:* "liked it to clarify what the user was trying to express"
    - *Con:* "didn't want to answer it but just wanted to talk directly about the issues"
  - **Bill's facial expression**
    - *Pro:* "make Bill's facial expression more affectionate, e.g., more smile" (Vet Center interview, 30-60 years old)
    - *Con:* "didn't want Bill become more affectionate which would be awkward" (Vet Center interview, 25-30 years old)
  - **Aggressive tone/choice of words**
    - *Pro:* "makes it seem more real and as a combat veteran I like it"
    - *Con:* "should adjust to the gender of the user"
  - **Link of SimCoach on the VA website**
    - *Pro:* "connect the Veteran's with appropriate providers and services"
    - *Con:* "The VA is not trust worthy"

Suggestions for Updates

Updates and Continuing Development

- **System update**
  - : Response time
  - : Speech recognition

  - − "Answer questions without such a long pause" (SA009)
  - − "Make the program voice activated. Typing sucks." (SA011)

Updates and Continuing Development

- **Program update**

  : Information (content): marriage, finance (home loan), military sexual trauma (w/ Elli)

  : Questionnaire during interaction: add some description to explain why users should take the questionnaire! (<- because some users wanted to skip it)

  - "Integrate a questionnaire prior to the SimCoach so Bill can be prompted to discuss key issues or focus on relevant topics." (VA014)
  - "I think it would improve if the SimCoach responses correlated with the person's responses." (COC3)
  - "I need a little more time to speak with him and to also look up the resources he gave to me to make sure it was the correct information." (VOALA11 & COC3)
  - "I wish that I had more information of what was available to me prior to starting. Perhaps more examples of how the system works or a brief video of a sample interplay with an individual showing how the exchange between Bill and the person would work." (SCUSVLB14)
  - "STRENGTHEN HIS (Bill's) KNOWLEDGE OF TEX-ABBRV. /TEX SHORTHAND" (SCUSVLB15)
  - "If comprehension issues are addressed this can potentially be a powerful tool." (SDAC4)
  - "I would like to see if they have way to talk about memory loss due to deployment." (VOALA11)
  - "The subject of MST or military sexual trauma should be included." (SCUSVLB16)
  - "By broadening the range of knowledge to accommodate potential questions based on common needs of veterans (i.e. housing, home loans, education assistant, credit repair, etc)" (NH003)

21   USC   ICT
                                                    INSTITUTE FOR CREATIVE TECHNOLOGIES

Updates and Continuing Development

- **Character update**
  : Consistency in responding to users' answers for the questions
  : More realistic character (vocabulary, facial expression, personality)

  - "create the avatar to be casual and respond back with sincerity." (VOALA15)

  - "I like it when the SimCoach cusses and uses words like shit and damn. Using cuss words makes it seem more real and as a combat veteran I like it when people are real and show their emotions when talking with them. Because physical expressions are difficult with technology, using words like this help. I think that having a counselor who smokes, dips, or has tattoos would also be helpful because I want to talk to someone who knows where I am coming from, not some guy in a sweater that analyzes everything I say." (SDAC3 & VA019)

  - "Depressed people can use some humor (so suggested to add humor or comedy to Bill)" (SCUSVLB interview)

  - "make Bill's facial expression more affectionate, e.g., smile more" (Vet Center interview)

  - " improve Bill's military acronym / jargon vocabulary and conversational style with regards to Vietnam" (Vet Center interview)

Updates and Continuing Development

- **Layout & Design update**
  - "I think it needs to be a bit more user friendly. The user has to look in 2 different places. Might be easier to type right into the conversation." (COC10)
  - "The users expressed that they had a difficult time watching the video and talk with Bill at the same time." (SCUSVLB interview)
  - "like to texting back and forth" (VOALA10)
  - "More flash and glitter" (SCUSVLB24)
  - "the boxes are too small and tab button should be able to move across" (COC interview)
  - "the video control buttons are not visible unless the cursor hovers over the video" (SCUSVLB interview)
  - "SimCoach's blue background seems very hospital like" (Vet Center interview)

- **Questions update**
  - "The options went from "sometimes" to "not at all" when asking about feelings of depression. This is a rather large gap and skims completely over any sort of "rarely" option."(COC1)
  - "I think that people should be able to write how they would like to answer Bills questions rather than have set answers to choose from." (COC9 & VOALA9)

ICT
INSTITUTE FOR CREATIVE TECHNOLOGIES

Further Work

Further Work

- **Further evaluation**
  - Longitudinal study
  - Evaluation with specifically targeted clinical group
  - Comparison between the SimCoach and other existing applications
  - HCI (Usability) experts' evaluation, e.g., Heuristic evaluation
  - Further qualitative evaluation, e.g., Think-Aloud evaluation

- **Any suggestion or questions?**

ICT
INSTITUTE FOR CREATIVE TECHNOLOGIES

Bibliography

"6 Simple Ways to Boost Concentration," *Natural Therapy Pages*, August 5, 2008. As of August 9, 2014:
http://www.naturaltherapypages.com.au/article/Poor_Concentration

American Academy of Sleep Medicine, "Sleep Hygiene: The Healthy Habits of Good Sleep," *Sleep Education*, undated.

Amstadter, Ananda B., Joshua Broman-Fulks, Heidi Zinzow, Kenneth J. Ruggiero, and Jen Cercone, "Internet-Based Interventions for Traumatic Stress–Related Mental Health Problems: A Review and Suggestion for Future Research," *Clinical Psychology Review*, Vol. 29, No. 5, July 2009, pp. 410–420.

Annon, Jack S., "The PLISSIT Model: A Proposed Conceptual Scheme for the Behavioral Treatment of Sexual Problems," *Journal of Sex Education and Therapy*, Vol. 2, No. 1, 1976, pp. 1–15.

———, "PLISSIT Therapy," in Raymond J. Corsini, ed., *Handbook of Innovative Psychotherapies*, New York: Wiley, 1981, pp. 626–639.

Barnes, Sean M., Kristen H. Walter, and Kathleen M. Chard, "Does a History of Mild Traumatic Brain Injury Increase Suicide Risk in Veterans with PTSD?" *Rehabilitation Psychology*, Vol. 57, No. 1, February 2012, pp. 18–26.

Bayir, Hülya, and Valerian E. Kagan, "Bench-to-Bedside Review: Mitochondrial Injury, Oxidative Stress and Apoptosis—There Is Nothing More Practical Than a Good Theory," *Critical Care*, Vol. 12, No. 1, February 2008, pp. 206–214.

Belasco, Amy, *The Cost of Iraq, Afghanistan, and Other Global War on Terror Operations Since 9/11*, Washington, D.C.: Congressional Research Service, RL33110, updated March 29, 2011. As of September 9, 2014:
http://www.fas.org/sgp/crs/natsec/RL33110.pdf

Blue, Laura, "Is Exercise the Best Drug for Depression?" *Time*, June 19, 2010.

Borzack, "Tips to Boost Energy and Stop Feeling Tired," *Healthy Lifestyle*, January 10, 2008. As of August 9, 2014:
http://healthy-lifestyle.most-effective-solution.com/2008/01/10/tips-to-boost-energy-and-stop-feeling-tired/

Britt, Thomas W., Tiffany M. Greene-Shortridge, Sarah Brink, Quyen B. Nguyen, Jaclyn Rath, Anthony L. Cox, Charles W. Hoge, and Carl Andrew Castro, "Perceived Stigma and Barriers to Care for Psychological Treatment: Implications for Reactions to Stressors in Different Contexts," *Journal of Social and Clinical Psychology*, Vol. 27, No. 4, 2008, pp. 317–335.

Bruce, Martha L., "Suicide Risk and Prevention in Veteran Populations," *Annals of the New York Academy of Sciences*, Vol. 1208, No. 1, 2010, pp. 98–103.

Bruner, Edward F., *Military Forces: What Is the Appropriate Size for the United States?* Washington, D.C.: Congressional Research Service, RS21754, updated January 24, 2006. As of September 9, 2014:
http://www.au.af.mil/au/awc/awcgate/crs/rs21754.pdf

Bryan, Craig J., and Tracy A. Clemans, "Repetitive Traumatic Brain Injury, Psychological Symptoms, and Suicide Risk in a Clinical Sample of Deployed Military Personnel," *JAMA Psychiatry*, Vol. 70, No. 7, 2013, pp. 686–691.

Campbell, Michelle, Ray Fitzpatrick, Andrew Haines, Ann Louise Kinmonth, Peter Sandercock, David Spiegelhalter, and Peter Tyrer, "Framework for Design and Evaluation of Complex Interventions to Improve Health," *BMJ*, Vol. 321, No. 7262, 2000, pp. 694–696.

Christensen, Helen, Liana S. Leach, Lisa Barney, Andrew J. Mackinnon, and Kathy M. Griffiths, "The Effect of Web Based Depression Interventions on Self Reported Help Seeking: Randomised Controlled Trial," *BMC Psychiatry*, Vol. 6, No. 13, 2006.

Committee on the Assessment of the Readjustment Needs of Military Personnel, Veterans, and Their Families, Board on the Health of Selected Populations, Institute of Medicine, *Returning Home from Iraq and Afghanistan: Assessment of Readjustment Needs of Veterans, Service Members, and Their Families*, Washington, D.C.: National Academies Press, 2013. As of August 6, 2014:
http://www.nap.edu/openbook.php?record_id=13499

Committee on the Initial Assessment of Readjustment Needs of Military Personnel, Veterans, and Their Families, Board on the Health of Selected Populations, Institute of Medicine, *Returning Home from Iraq and Afghanistan: Preliminary Assessment of Readjustment Needs of Veterans, Service Members, and Their Families*, Washington, D.C.: National Academies Press, 2010. As of August 6, 2014:
http://www.nap.edu/openbook.php?record_id=12812

Community Preventive Services Task Force, "Preventing Excessive Alcohol Consumption: Electronic Screening and Brief Interventions (e-SBI): Task Force Finding and Rationale Statement," *The Guide to Community Preventive Services*, review completed 2012; page last reviewed September 24, 2013. As of March 20, 2014:
http://www.thecommunityguide.org/alcohol/RReSBI.html

Defense Health Services Systems Program Executive Office, *Contingency Tracking System (CTS) Interface Control Document (ICD) Describing Data Exchange to the MDR Baseline*, Falls Church, Va., April 12, 2012. As of August 6, 2014:
http://tricare.mil/tma/dhcape/data/downloads/ICDs/ICD%201300-7001-03%20Approved%20CTS.docx

Defense Manpower Data Center, *Contingency Tracking System (CTS) Deployment File Baseline Report (as of December 31, 2012)*, c. 2013.

Donkin, Liesje, Ian B. Hickie, Helen Christensen, Sharon L. Naismith, Bruce Neal, Nicole L. Cockayne, and Nick Glozier, "Rethinking the Dose–Response Relationship Between Usage and Outcome in an Online Intervention for Depression: Randomized Controlled Trial," *Journal of Medical Internet Research*, Vol. 15, No. 10, 2013, p. e231.

Dy, Sydney M., Stephanie L. Taylor, Lauren H. Carr, Robbie Foy, Peter J. Pronovost, John Ovretveit, Robert M. Wachter, Lisa V. Rubenstein, Susanne Hempel, Kathryn M. McDonald, and Paul G. Shekelle, "A Framework for Classifying Patient Safety Practices: Results from an Expert Consensus Process," *BMJ Quality and Safety*, Vol. 20, No. 7, July 2011, pp. 618–624.

"Fatigue," *MedlinePlus*, updated April 21, 2013. As of August 9, 2014:
http://www.nlm.nih.gov/medlineplus/ency/article/003088.htm

Forbes, David, Mark Creamer, Jonathan I. Bisson, Judith A. Cohen, Bruce E. Crow, Edna B. Foa, Matthew J. Friedman, Terence M. Keane, Harold S. Kudler, and Robert J. Ursano, "A Guide to Guidelines for the Treatment of PTSD and Related Conditions," *Journal of Traumatic Stress*, Vol. 23, No. 5, October 2010, pp. 537–552.

Green, Jackie, "The Role of Theory in Evidence-Based Health Promotion Practice," *Health Education Research*, Vol. 15, No. 2, April 2000, pp. 125–129.

Gulliver, Amelia, Kathleen M. Griffiths, Helen Christensen, and Jacqueline L. Brewer, "A Systematic Review of Help-Seeking Interventions for Depression, Anxiety and General Psychological Distress," *BMC Psychiatry*, Vol. 12, No. 1, 2012, p. 81.

Hoge, Charles W., Jennifer L. Auchterlonie, and Charles S. Milliken, "Mental Health Problems, Use of Mental Health Services, and Attrition from Military Service After Returning from Deployment to Iraq or Afghanistan," *Journal of the American Medical Association*, Vol. 295, No. 9, March 1, 2006, pp. 1023–1032.

Hoge, Charles W., Carl A. Castro, Stephen C. Messer, Dennis McGurk, Dave I. Cotting, and Robert L. Koffman, "Combat Duty in Iraq and Afghanistan, Mental Health Problems, and Barriers to Care," *New England Journal of Medicine*, Vol. 351, No. 1, July 1, 2004, pp. 13–22.

Hoge, Charles W., Dennis McGurk, Jeffrey L. Thomas, Anthony L. Cox, Charles C. Engel, and Carl A. Castro, "Mild Traumatic Brain Injury in U.S. Soldiers Returning from Iraq," *New England Journal of Medicine*, Vol. 358, No. 5, January 31, 2008, pp. 453–463.

Houston, Thomas K., Julie E. Volkman, Hua Feng, Kim M. Nazi, Stephanie L. Shimada, and Susannah Fox, "Veteran Internet Use and Engagement with Health Information Online," *Military Medicine*, Vol. 178, No. 4, April 2013, pp. 394–400.

ICT—*See* University of Southern California Institute for Creative Technologies.

John, Bruce S., Stephanie Smolinski, Julia Kim, Albert Rizzo, and J. Galen Buckwalter, "Administering a Standard Mental Health Questionnaire Through a Virtual Human: Comparisons with a Conversational Version of the PHQ-9," unpublished manuscript, 2011.

Kenny, Patrick, Arno Hartholt, Jonathan Gratch, William Swartout, David Traum, Stacy Marsella, and Diane Piepol, "Building Interactive Virtual Humans for Training Environments," *Interservice/Industry Training, Simulation, and Education Conference (I/ITSEC) 2007*, paper 7105, 2007. As of August 6, 2014: http://ict.usc.edu/pubs/ Building%20Interactive%20Virtual%20Humans%20for%20Training%20Environments.pdf

Kim, Paul Y., Thomas W. Britt, Robert P. Klocko, Lyndon A. Riviere, and Amy B. Adler, "Stigma, Negative Attitudes About Treatment, and Utilization of Mental Health Care Among Soldiers," *Military Psychology*, Vol. 23, No. 1, January 2011, pp. 65–81.

Kroenke, Kurt, Robert L. Spitzer, and Janet B. Williams, "The PHQ-9: Validity of a Brief Depression Severity Measure," *Journal of General Internal Medicine*, Vol. 16, No. 9, September 2001, pp. 606–613.

———, "The Patient Health Questionnaire–2: Validity of a Two-Item Depression Screener," *Medical Care*, Vol. 41, No. 11, November 2003, pp. 1284–1292.

Lalkhen, Abdul Ghaaliq, and Anthony McCluskey, "Clinical Tests: Sensitivity and Specificity," *Continuing Education in Anaesthesia, Critical Care and Pain*, Vol. 8, No. 6, 2008, pp. 221–223.

Lang, Ariel J., and Murray B. Stein, "An Abbreviated PTSD Checklist for Use as a Screening Instrument in Primary Care," *Behaviour Research and Therapy*, Vol. 43, No. 5, May 2005, pp. 585–594.

Lang, Ariel J., K. Wilkins, P. P. Roy-Byrne, D. Golinelli, D. Chavira, C. Sherbourne, R. D. Rose, A. Bystritsky, G. Sullivan, M. G. Craske, and M. B. Stein, "Abbreviated PTSD Checklist (PCL) as a Guide to Clinical Response," *General Hospital Psychiatry*, Vol. 34, No. 4, July–August 2012, pp. 332–338.

Lee, Jina, and Stacy Marsella, "Nonverbal Behavior Generator for Embodied Conversational Agents," *Intelligent Virtual Agents*, Vol. 4133, 2006, pp. 243–255.

Lee, Scott, "Memories, Flashbacks and Dissociation as a Function of Combat PTSD/TBI: Experiential Research," *PTSD: A Soldier's Perspective*, June 5, 2011. As of August 9, 2014: http://ptsdasoldiersperspective.blogspot.com/2011/06/memories-flashbacks-and-dissociation-as.html

Liu, Chao, Ryen W. White, and Susan Dumais, "Understanding Web Browsing Behaviors Through Weibull Analysis of Dwell Time," *SIGIR'10*, July 19–23, 2010, pp. 379–386. As of August 6, 2014: http://research.microsoft.com/en-us/um/people/ryenw/papers/liusigir2010.pdf

Management of Major Depressive Disorder Working Group, *VA/DoD Clinical Practice Guideline for the Management of Major Depressive Disorder*, Washington, D.C., 2009. As of August 6, 2014: http://www.guideline.gov/content.aspx?id=15675

Marsella, Stacy C., W. Lewis Johnson, and Catherine M. LaBore, "Interactive Pedagogical Drama for Health Interventions," *11th International Conference on Artificial Intelligence in Education*, Sydney, Australia, 2003, pp. 341–348.

Miller, William R., and Stephen Rollnick, *Motivational Interviewing: Preparing People to Change Addictive Behavior*, New York: Guilford Press, 1991.

Morbini, Fabrizio, Eric Forbell, David DeVault, Kenji Sagae, David R. Traum, and Albert A. Rizzo, "A Mixed-Initiative Conversational Dialogue System for Healthcare," *Proceedings of the 13th Annual Meeting of the Special Interest Group on Discourse and Dialogue*, 2012, pp. 137–139.

Morie, Jacquelyn Ford, Eric Chance, Kip Haynes, and Dinesh Rajpurohit, "Embodied Conversational Agent Avatars in Virtual Worlds: Making Today's Immersive Environments More Responsive to Participants," in Philip Hingston, ed., *Believable Bots: Can Computers Play Like People?* Springer, 2012, pp. 99–118.

Mouthaan, Joanne, Marit Sijbrandij, Giel-Jan de Vries, Johannes B. Reitsma, Rens van de Schoot, J. Carel Goslings, Jan S. K. Luitse, Fred C. Bakker, Berthold P. R. Gersons, and Miranda Olff, "Internet-Based Early Intervention to Prevent Posttraumatic Stress Disorder in Injury Patients: Randomized Controlled Trial," *Journal of Medical Internet Research*, Vol. 15, No. 8, 2013, pp. e165–e176.

National Center for PTSD, title unknown, date unknown. No longer online.

———, "PTSD: National Center for PTSD," undated; referenced August 27, 2013. As of August 6, 2014: http://www.ptsd.va.gov/

———, "Relationships and PTSD," last updated January 3, 2014. As of August 9, 2014: http://www.ptsd.va.gov/public/family/ptsd-and-relationships.asp

Orvis, Karin A., Jennifer C. Moore, James Belanich, Jennifer S. Murphy, and Daniel B. Horn, "Are Soldiers Gamers? Videogame Usage Among Soldiers and Implications for the Effective Use of Serious Videogames for Military Training," *Military Psychology*, Vol. 22, No. 2, April–June 2010, pp. 143–157.

Pietrzak, Robert H., Douglas C. Johnson, Marc B. Goldstein, James C. Malley, and Steven M. Southwick, "Perceived Stigma and Barriers to Mental Health Care Utilization Among OEF-OIF Veterans," *Psychiatric Services*, Vol. 60, No. 8, August 2009, pp. 1118–1122.

Prochaska, James O., and Carlo C. DiClemente, "Transtheoretical Therapy: Toward a More Integrative Model of Change," *Psychotherapy: Theory, Research and Practice*, Vol. 19, No. 3, 1982, pp. 276–288.

Ramchand, Rajeev, Terry L. Schell, Benjamin R. Karney, Karen Chan Osilla, Rachel M. Burns, and Leah Barnes Caldarone, "Disparate Prevalence Estimates of PTSD Among Service Members Who Served in Iraq and Afghanistan: Possible Explanations," *Journal of Traumatic Stress*, Vol. 23, No. 1, February 2010, pp. 59–68.

Reins, Jo Annika, David Daniel Ebert, Dirk Lehr, Heleen Riper, Pim Cuijpers, and Matthias Berking, "Internet-Based Treatment of Major Depression for Patients on a Waiting List for Inpatient Psychotherapy: Protocol for a Multi-Centre Randomised Controlled Trial," *BMC Psychiatry*, Vol. 13, 2013, p. 318.

Rizzo, Albert, J. Galen Buckwalter, Eric Forbell, Chris Reist, JoAnn Difede, Barbara O. Rothbaum, Belinda Lange, Sebastian Koenig, and Thomas Talbot, "Virtual Reality Applications to Address the Wounds of War," *Psychiatric Annals*, Vol. 43, No. 3, March 2013, pp. 123–138.

Rizzo, Albert A., Jon Gratch, Julia Kim, and Stacy Marsella, "SimCoach: Promoting Healthcare Outreach and Advocacy with Virtual Humans," proposal, Marina del Rey, Calif.: University of Southern California, Institute for Creative Technologies, 2009.

Rizzo, Albert A., Belinda Lange, John G. Buckwalter, Eric Forbell, Julia Kim, Kenji Sagae, Josh Williams, Barbara O. Rothbaum, JoAnn Difede, Greg Reger, Thomas Parsons, and Patrick Kenny, "An Intelligent Virtual Human System for Providing Healthcare Information and Support," in James D. Westwood, Susan W. Westwood, Li Fellander-Tsai, Randy S. Haluck, Helene M. Hoffman, Richard A. Robb, Steven Senger, and Kirby G. Vosburgh, eds., *Medicine Meets Virtual Reality 18: NextMed*, Amsterdam: IOS Press, 2011, pp. 503–509.

Rizzo, Albert A., Kenji Sagae, Eric Forbell, Julia Kim, Belinda Lange, John Galen Buckwalter, Josh Williams, Thomas D. Parsons, Patrick Kenny, and David Traum, "SimCoach: An Intelligent Virtual Human System for Providing Healthcare Information and Support," *Interservice/Industry Training, Simulation, and Education Conference (I/ITSEC) 2011*, Orlando, Fla., paper 11263, 2011.

Rosenthal, Michele, "Treating PTSD: Taking Control of the Picture," *Heal My PTSD*, August 19, 2009. No longer online.

Sagae, Kenji, Gwen Christian, David DeVault, and David R. Traum, "Towards Natural Language Understanding of Partial Speech Recognition Results in Dialogue Systems," *Proceedings of Human Language Technologies: The 2009 Annual Conference of the North American Chapter of the Association for Computational Linguistics*, Companion Volume: *Short Papers*, 2009, pp. 53–56.

Scott, John M., David A. Wheeler, Mark Lucas, and J. C. Herz, *Open Technology Development (ODT): Lessons Learned and Best Practices for Military Software*, Washington, D.C.: U.S. Department of Defense, May 16, 2011. As of August 6, 2014:
http://dodcio.defense.gov/Portals/0/Documents/FOSS/OTD-lessons-learned-military-signed.pdf

"Screening, Brief Intervention and Referral to Treatment (SBIRT) in Behavioral Healthcare," unpublished white paper, April 1, 2011. As of August 21, 2014:
http://beta.samhsa.gov/sites/default/files/sbirtwhitepaper_0.pdf

Seal, K. H., D. Bertenthal, C. R. Miner, S. Sen, and C. Marmar, "Bringing the War Back Home: Mental Health Disorders Among 103,788 US Veterans Returning from Iraq and Afghanistan Seen at Department of Veterans Affairs Facilities," *Archives of Internal Medicine*, Vol. 167, No. 5, March 12, 2007, pp. 476–482.

Serafino, Nina M., *Peacekeeping and Related Stability Operations: Issues of U.S. Military Involvement*, Washington, D.C.: Congressional Research Service, IB94040, updated September 15, 2005.

Shiner, Brian, "Health Services Use in the Department of Veterans Affairs Among Returning Iraq War and Afghan War Veterans with PTSD," *PTSD Research Quarterly*, Vol. 22, No. 2, 2011, pp. 1–10. As of September 9, 2011:
http://www.ptsd.va.gov/professional/newsletters/research-quarterly/v22n2.pdf

SimCoach Team in MedVR Group, *SimCoach Onsite Evaluation: Preliminary Results*, U.S. Army, January 19, 2012.

Smith, T. C., D. L. Wingard, M. A. K. Ryan, D. Kritz-Silverstein, D. J. Slymen, and J. F. Sallis, "Prior Assault and Posttraumatic Stress Disorder After Combat Deployment," *Epidemiology*, Vol. 19, No. 3, May 2008, pp. 505–512.

State Government of Victoria, "Fatigue Fighting Tips," *Better Health Channel*, last reviewed December 2011. As of August 9, 2014:
http://www.betterhealth.vic.gov.au/bhcv2/bhcarticles.nsf/pages/Fatigue_fighting_tips

Stecker, Tracy, John C. Fortney, Francis Hamilton, and Icek Ajzen, "An Assessment of Beliefs About Mental Health Care Among Veterans Who Served in Iraq," *Psychiatric Services*, Vol. 58, No. 10, October 1, 2007, pp. 1358–1361.

Stecker, Tracy, Brian Shiner, Bradley V. Watts, Meissa Jones, and Kenneth R. Conner, "Treatment-Seeking Barriers for Veterans of the Iraq and Afghanistan Conflicts Who Screen Positive for PTSD," *Psychiatric Services*, Vol. 64, No. 3, March 2013, pp. 280–283.

Swartout, William, Ron Artstein, Eric Forbell, Susan Foutz, H. Chad Lane, Belinda Lange, Jacquelyn Ford Morie, Albert Skip Rizzo, and David Traum, "Virtual Humans for Learning," *AI Magazine*, Vol. 34, No. 4, 2013, pp. 13–30.

Tanielian, Terri, and Lisa H. Jaycox, eds., *Invisible Wounds of War: Psychological and Cognitive Injuries, Their Consequences, and Services to Assist Recovery*, Santa Monica, Calif.: RAND Corporation, MG-720-CCF, 2008. As of August 6, 2014:
http://www.rand.org/pubs/monographs/MG720.html

Thiebaux, Marcus, Stacy Marsella, Andrew N. Marshall, and Marcelo Kallmann, "SmartBody: Behavior Realization for Embodied Conversational Agents," *Proceedings of the 7th International Joint Conference on Autonomous Agents and Multiagent Systems*, Vol. 1, 2008, pp. 151–158.

Tull, Matthew, "Coping with Flashbacks," *About.com*, updated June 11, 2014. As of August 9, 2014:
http://ptsd.about.com/od/selfhelp/a/flashcoping.htm

University of Southern California Institute for Creative Technologies, "SimCoach," undated; referenced September 9, 2014. As of October 10, 2014:
http://ict.usc.edu/prototypes/simcoach/

U.S. Department of Veterans Affairs, "VA/DoD Clinical Practice Guidelines: Management of Post-Traumatic Stress Disorder and Acute Stress Reaction (2010)," 2010; referenced May 29, 2013. As of August 6, 2014: http://www.healthquality.va.gov/Post_Traumatic_Stress_Disorder_PTSD.asp

VA—*See* U.S. Department of Veterans Affairs.

Van Rosmalen-Nooijens, Karin A. W. L., Judith B. Prins, Marianne Vergeer, Sylvie H. Lo Fo Wong, and Antoine L. M. Lagro-Janssen, "'Young People, Adult Worries': RCT of an Internet-Based Self-Support Method 'Feel the ViBe' for Children, Adolescents and Young Adults Exposed to Family Violence, a Study Protocol," *BMC Public Health*, Vol. 13, 2013, p. 226

Vannoy, Steven D., Tonya Fancher, Caitlyn Meltvedt, Jürgen Unützer, Paul Duberstein, and Richard L. Kravitz, "Suicide Inquiry in Primary Care: Creating Context, Inquiring, and Following Up," *Annals of Family Medicine*, Vol. 8, No. 1, January–February 2010, pp. 33–39.

Vasterling, Jennifer J., Susan P. Proctor, Matthew J. Friedman, Charles W. Hoge, Timothy Heeren, Lynda A. King, and Daniel W. King, "PTSD Symptom Increases in Iraq-Deployed Soldiers: Comparison with Nondeployed Soldiers and Associations with Baseline Symptoms, Deployment Experiences, and Postdeployment Stress," *Journal of Traumatic Stress*, Vol. 23, No. 1, February 2010, pp. 41–51.

Vogt, Dawne, "Mental Health–Related Beliefs as a Barrier to Service Use for Military Personnel and Veterans: A Review," *Psychiatric Services*, Vol. 62, No. 2, February 2011, pp. 135–142.

Vogt, Dawne, Amy Bergeron, Dawn Salgado, Jennifer Daley, Paige Ouimette, and Jessica Wolfe, "Barriers to Veterans Health Administration Care in a Nationally Representative Sample of Women Veterans," *Journal of General Internal Medicine*, Vol. 21, No. 3 Suppl., March 2006, pp. S19–S25.

Walters, Scott T., Elizabeth Miller, and Emil Chiauzzi, "Wired for Wellness: E-Interventions for Addressing College Drinking," *Journal of Substance Abuse Treatment*, Vol. 29, No. 2, September 2005, pp. 139–145.

Wilson, Coralie J., Frank P. Deane, and Joseph Ciarrochi, "Measuring Help-Seeking Intentions: Properties of the General Help-Seeking Questionnaire," *Canadian Journal of Counselling*, Vol. 39, No. 1, January 2005, pp. 15–28.